MOVEMENT ACTIVITIES, MOTOR ABILITY AND THE EDUCATION OF CHILDREN

MOVEMENT ACTIVITIES, MOTOR ABILITY AND THE EDUCATION OF CHILDREN

By

BRYANT J. CRATTY, Ed.D.
Professor of Physical Education
University of California
Los Angeles, California

NAMIKO IKEDA, Ph.D.
Associate Professor of Physical Education
Slippery Rock State College
Slippery Rock, Pennsylvania

SISTER MARGARET MARY MARTIN, M.S.
Chairman, Department of Physical Education
Alverno College
Milwaukee, Wisconsin

CLAIR JENNETT, Ph.D.
Professor of Physical Education
California State College
San Jose, California

MARGARET MORRIS, Ph.D.
Professor of Physical Education
Eastern Oregon State College
La Grande, Oregon

CHARLES C THOMAS • PUBLISHER
Springfield • Illinois • U.S.A.

Published and Distributed Throughout the World by
CHARLES C THOMAS • PUBLISHER

BANNERSTONE HOUSE
301-327 East Lawrence Avenue, Springfield, Illinois, U.S.A.
NATCHEZ PLANTATION HOUSE
735 North Atlantic Boulevard, Fort Lauderdale, Florida, U.S.A.

With THOMAS BOOKS *careful attention is given to all details of
manufacturing and design. It is the Publisher's desire to present books
that are satisfactory as to their physical qualities and artistic possibilities
and appropriate for their particular use.* THOMAS BOOKS *will be true
to those laws of quality that assure a good name and good will.*

Printed in the United States of America
W-2

INTRODUCTION

W ITHIN THE EDUCATIONAL environment the child presents two primary facets of his personality to those who take the time to observe. Sometimes he is passive, contemplative and relatively immobile; he is engaged in thought. At other times he is in action; he runs from class to class and engages in vigorous active games with his friends on the playground.

A problem that has plagued philosophers for years, however, is just how discrete are these two components of the child's behavior. On one hand are those who suggest that the human animal may be neatly fragmented into spiritual, physical, emotional and cognitive components. While on the other hand there are those who in a rather sweeping manner declare that the child is an undifferentiated whole whose mental, motor, religious and affective behaviors are so overlapping as to be indivisible.

The writers of this text believe that both of these viewpoints are simplistic to the extreme, and are not very helpful when attempting to delineate the exact manner in which one facet of a child's personality interacts with other components. Rather, the authors hold that the young *homo sapiens* is an extremely complex assemblage of attributes, and that the global suggestion that he is comprised of a single "lump" of characteristics, or that he may be neatly compartmentalized, is not as fruitful as attempting to delineate just how emotion is reflected in physiological changes, how the manner in which motor proficiency (or ineptitude) may modify social functioning, or how certain perceptual or cognitive attributes may be adjusted with certain kinds of specific movement experiences.

It is believed that the vast amount of data emanating from studies of human development and behavior suggests that indeed at times the various components of the human personality overlap and interrelate in reasonably predictable ways, while at other times ability traits may function in rather independent ways. For example, a child may sit and think without there being any observable experimental and observational evidence suggesting that movement is occurring in his larger skeletal muscles; while at other times the same child may be thinking a great deal about the proper rules or strategies to apply while running rapidly in a playground game. To cite another example, it is apparent that to intercept balls in various sports activities certain visual-perceptual attributes must be intact. However, the research makes it equally clear that many individuals are able to evidence rather sophisticated sets of visual-perceptual attributes which are not only independent of each other, but at the same time have not apparently arisen from nor depend upon the capacity to move effectively.*

Despite the apparent attempt to reduce the importance of movement within the structure of the personality evident in the preceding statements, the authors of this text feel that indeed the obvious expressive facets of the child's character are extremely important to consider when attempting to effect some type of change within various types of educational environments. It is felt, however, that the manner in which movement experiences, or attempts to reduce extraneous movement, may contribute or detract from other goals educators set for themselves and for their charges must be clearly spelled out. If possible, it is believed that reasonably sound data should be collected which delineate in rather specific ways just how, for example, being clumsy may affect a child's self-concept, or how children with learning difficulties may benefit from or be impeded by participation in various kinds of learning games.

It was with these kinds of questions in mind that the experiments reported on the following pages were initiated. For the most part they were carried out during the school year of 1969-1970 in the Perceptual-Motor Learning Laboratory at the University of California at Los Angeles by the director, his administrative assistant, and three postdoctoral students who were

---

* The reader is referred to *Perceptual and Motor Development In Children* (New York, Macmillan, 1970), by the first author, for a more complete and well-documented development of these postulates.

present at that time. The research was financed by a private donor's grant.

Four experiments are reported on the pages which follow. In one it was attempted to determine the degree to which change in selected motor and perceptual attributes could be expected to occur, following a program of remediation in which children with perceptual-motor difficulties participated. Collection of the data in this investigation was supervised by Dr. Namiko Ikeda, and she was assisted by Mr. Larry Rothstein. The findings were highly promising and suggested that in addition to selected basic motor ability traits, certain perceptual attributes may be modified by a properly applied program of motor activity. The drawback to the investigation was the fact that the so-called controls were not well matched in motor ability to the children in the experimental group. It is hoped that this deficiency will be rectified in future investigations.

Another study reported was supervised by Sister Margaret Mary Martin. Additionally, she taught the experimental program which was applied to twenty-eight children (25 of whom were Negro) who evidenced pronounced learning difficulties in the early elementary school years and whose average I.Q. was 75. This study was based upon the proposition that to aid children to acquire certain academic processes through movement, one must rather exactly combine movement activities with those same processes instead of hoping for some kind of magic transfer to occur from balance beam walking to reading. With this in mind, a series of movement activities purporting to enhance attention and impulse control, pattern and letter recognition, as well as serial memory ability and spelling, was included in a seventeen-week program. As in the first study reviewed, the findings emanating from this second one were promising. The children evidenced marked improvement in a variety of classroom operations, including the ability to remember more things in a series, to recognize letters and to evidence better self-control. Even the more retarded children improved in the expected directions. However, this investigation represents merely a pilot effort and lacked any control for the innumerable variables which might have influenced the test scores collected following the application of the program. Such factors as the personality of the instructor, learning to take the tests, the release from classroom tensions, and the motivating effect of the games will be controlled in an investigation begun in September 1969 and financed by the U.S. Department of Education.

It is believed that the findings arising from the studies of the self-concept and game choices of children with motor problems are highly illuminating. They reflect, for example, that the clumsy boy is probably compensating in a number of ways for his ineptitude. For example, he seems, as would be expected, to be avoiding vigorous, active games and, well into late childhood, engaging in a great deal of fantasy play in which some kind of "cowboy," "spaceman," or "cops and robbers" hero is involved. This same boy seems also to be incurring a great number of problems in social interactions with his peers. He will admit that he has trouble making friends, that his friends make fun of him, and that boys dislike him to a far greater degree than they do boys with game skills. These data perhaps just confirm what most parents and some educators have observed for years, but at the same time these investigations offer insight into the problems incurred by boys who cannot compete physically and socially with their peers.

The remaining parts of the text contain essays on cognition, motor learning, and the manner in which activity arousal level may detract and/or enhance intellectual functioning.

The authors appreciate very much the opportunity extended to them by the Publisher to present their research in book form. Research articles around the turn of the century, while using few subjects and evidencing little statistical sophistication, contained extensive essays expounding and elaborating on the data that were collected. More contemporary articles have often consisted of rather an extensive number of statistical tables, but little discussion of the findings or of their implications. We are grateful to the Publisher for the exposure given the data we collected and for the opportunity to examine and explore our findings. Numbers need explanations; from statistics should come ideas, and from ideas stem not only further productive research but, hopefully, rewarding changes in the manner in which the components of educational programs are selected and applied.

ACKNOWLEDGMENTS

THE AUTHORS WOULD like to thank the contributors to the private donor's grant which made much of this research possible, and also Mrs. Marell Malak, Principal of Fairburn Elementary School in Los Angeles, and Dr. Frank Taylor, Supervisor of Special Education in the City of Santa Monica, California, for their cooperation and their permission to test subjects within their institutions. Their staffs, whose schedules were often disrupted by our investigators, are also extended thanks.

We are indebted to Monsignor James B. Clyne, superintendent of the Elementary Schools in the Catholic Archdiocese of Los Angeles, for permission to conduct the pilot study in an inner city school of the archdiocese. We wish to thank: Sister Rosemary Sanford, the principal of St. Malachy Elementary School, for her cooperation; Sister Marie Louise Gomez, Mrs. Rosalie Alexander, Mrs. Audrey Baquet, and Mrs. Claire Frazier for adjusting their class schedules to meet the needs of the investigator of the study.

Mr. Jeffrey Drucker aided in the typing of the manuscript and in the drawing of the graphs. Mrs. Anna Carrillo, Miss Sara Dobbins and Miss Jill Woodmansee contributed a great deal to the manuscript with their clerical and editorial skills. To these four people the authors are grateful.

CONTENTS

MOVEMENT ACTIVITIES, MOTOR ABILITY AND THE EDUCATION OF CHILDREN

PART ONE
RESEARCH STUDIES

Chapter I

THE SELF-CONCEPT OF CHILDREN WITH COORDINATION PROBLEMS

INTRODUCTION AND REVIEW OF THE LITERATURE

MUCH OF THE literature dealing with the self-concept of adults and children during the past years has received impetus both from Carl Rogers' self-theory and from Freud's concept of the ego (13). Rogers, for example, suggests that personal adjustment is to a large degree dependent upon the formation of a valid self-concept which leads toward self-acceptance (25).

During the 1950's several attempts were made to evaluate the self-concept in college-age youth using questionnaire methods. Although studies by Coppersmith (5), Perkins (22) and Sears (27) attempted to evaluate certain aspects of the self-concept in children, their attempts have been criticized for the lack of standardization, poor validation of the instruments used (12) and for the lack of prolonged investigation of feelings which are likely to be relatively transitory in children and youth (23).

Physical educators have attempted at times to dissect components of the self-concept. They have sometimes been concerned with specific measures of the body image, using projective tests as well as direct self-reporting methods (2, 28). Much of their work in this problem area has been inspired by Schilder's classic text (26).

Another component of the "physical self-concept" which has been explored experimentally is represented by various studies of a) self-estimations of performance scores and b) aspiration level in successively administered motor tasks of various kinds. Studies of this nature have been reviewed by Cratty (7) and by Inglis (17). The measures obtained from investigations of this

5

nature include discrepancies between the individual's estimation of future performance and actual performance as well as the number of times estimates fluctuate over and under future performances due to exceeding or not reaching previous estimates.

Numerous measures, varying in objectivity, have been utilized to evaluate the body image, including projective measures (15), various draw-a-person tests (30), direct polling involving body-part identification (2), manikin construction tests (1), stated feelings about various body parts (28), and scores derived from the accuracy with which a child imitates simple and complex gestures of the examiner (3). These techniques have been recently reviewed and evaluated in a monograph (11) and a book (9) by the first author.

Until the early 1960's no reliable evaluation instruments had been developed, however, which permitted more than a cursory estimate of how children feel about their general physical appearance and their ability to perform physical skills. To fill this need, Ellen Piers and Dale Harris, at Pennsylvania State University in 1964, constructed a self-concept test (23). The final scale of items was gleaned from an original pool of 164 statements which were obtained from Jersild's collection of children's statements concerning what they liked and disliked about themselves (18). The statements from the Piers-Harris Scale which are indicative of the child's feelings about his physical ability and appearance were those employed in this investigation. A more thorough description of the manner in which this instrument was constructed is found in the section which follows, dealing with procedures.

Changes in young men's stated feelings about their bodies and performance capacities have been studied by Gasser in 1967 (14). He found that following a program of weight training, a heightened self-concept was reflected in a questionnaire specifically constructed for the investigation.* Clifton and Smith completed studies which revealed that college women and men evidenced significant positive changes in self-assessments of

---

* Test-retest reliability ranged from .87 to .94.

physical ability after viewing themselves executing a throwing movement (4).

Read, in a recent investigation, explored the influence of competitive and noncompetitive programs of physical education upon the self-concept of sixty-nine high school juniors. He found, as would be expected, that consistent losers had a lower self-concept than consistent winners (24). Read employed the Tennessee self-concept scale in his work.

Thus it is apparent that with the opportunity to view one's movement, to experience success or failure in motor performance as well as perceived changes in physical capacities, the feelings late adolescents and young adults have about selected components of self-concept may be altered.

Review of the literature revealed few studies in which the self-concept of children was evaluated with reference to feelings associated with physical activity (22, 27). One of these, a correlative study, deals directly with what was termed "self-esteem" as related to physical fitness and attitudes toward physical activity (29). The findings of this latter study reveal low-moderate correlations between fitness levels and self-esteem. The previously mentioned investigation by Piers and Harris resulted in findings that the self-concept score obtained bore a low relationship to I.Q. ($r=+.23$ and $+.32$); had good internal consistency, as evaluated on the Kuder-Richardson Index; and the test-retest reliability, interpolated by a four-month period, was fair ($r=.72$). A factor analysis revealed six interpretable factors, one of which (physical appearance and attributes) contained several of the items employed on the final scale used in this investigation. The remainder of the items for the test employed in this study were selected arbitrarily from this same list. The scale employed for this investigation (see Appendix) has been used in previous studies reported in texts by Cratty (8) and by Cratty and Martin (10). In general, it was found in these investigations that while the physical ability of neurologically impaired children and retarded children may be significantly altered over a five-month period, marked changes in reported self-concept obtained from these same populations on a five-month pre-posttest situation were not significant. It was concluded, however, that the scale employed was potentially useful as an evaluative instrument. Work with this scale revealed that its usefulness was limited if the intelligence quotient of the respondents was less than 70 or if the chronological age of normal subjects was under six years.

Purpose

The investigation reported on the following pages had as its purpose the collection of normative data using the questions from the Piers-Harris Scale, which purportedly evaluates physical ability and attributes. It was intended further to survey both sex and age differences revealed in responses to the questionnaire. It was assumed that when valid norms are obtained, viable inferences may be made when similar responses are collected from individuals and from groups of atypical children. For example, the second part of the investigation presents a comparison of responses obtained from 132 children classified as minimally neurologically handicapped, to responses obtained from the normal population surveyed in this investigation.

When further data of this nature are obtained, an item analysis should result in helpful modifications of the test content.

Significance of the Study

It is believed that self-concept and possible changes elicited therein are important variables to consider when studies are carried out in which it is hypothesized that some program of physical activity will modify some intellectual or academic component of the child's personality. Weatherford, for example, suggests that academic achievement is related to optimum levels of peer acceptance (31). Oliver attributed the I.Q. score changes of 25 percent which he obtained in educable retardates to positive shifts in their self-concept. These changes were due, Oliver suggested, to perceived changes in physical capabilities which resulted from a vigorous program of physical education he had instituted (21). Gorlow *et al.* produced findings which indicate that the self-concept of retardates is generally low (16). While evidence obtained in a 1966 study by Cratty revealed that the presence of what was termed a "failure syndrome" tended to "blunt" the performance scores of retardates in physical tasks in late childhood, due to feelings of failure engendered prior to that time (6).

It is thus hoped that further refinement of scales such as the one utilized in this investigation might result in more penetrating approaches to the study of the effects of physical performance changes upon fluctuations in measures of mental, emotional and/or academic traits.

Many critical questions, of course, permeate this type of investigation, including the following: Are there age and sex differences in the extent to which physical capacity contributes to the self-concept? Why do previous studies sometimes show physical performance changes without the expected changes in self-concept scores? Must transfer from physical improvement to self-concept be taught? (i.e. "Look, Johnny, how much you have improved your score!") And most important, just how much of the child's total self-concept is dependent upon his proficiency in motor skills and in group games?

PROCEDURES

In 1967 a battery of motor and psychological tests were established in the Perceptual-Motor Learning Laboratory at UCLA with which to evaluate children referred for remedial education. A portion of this battery of tests was devoted to paper and pencil measures of game-choice (gender identification) and self-concept in children. When attempting to obtain the tools with which to measure the self-concept quality in children, our attention was directed toward the work of Piers and Harris completed in 1967. Correspondence with Dr. Ellen Piers resulted in the receipt of a list of questions from their test of self-concept which purportedly evaluates a child's feelings about his physical ability and appearance. Some of these questions were selected for the modified battery used in this study. This direct questionnaire measure was thus included in the one-hour evaluation for the next several years, and during that time the responses of approximately 350 children were polled.

The results of two preliminary analyses of the data are contained in two texts, by Cratty (8) and by Cratty and Martin (10). The purpose of these two pilot studies was to determine if shifts in mean scores and in percentage of positive responses to the various questions occurred following participation in a five-month program of perceptual-motor training. In general, the findings from these investigations indicated that while significant changes in scores reflecting perceptual and motor attributes occurred during this period of time, few significant changes were recorded by either retarded or normal (clumsy) children when their self-concept scores were compared. Lacking in this investigation were any reliable scores obtained from normal populations of children, so that evaluation of the self-concept scores obtained from the two groups of atypical children was difficult.

In the spring of 1969 Dr. Clair Jennett obtained data, using the questionnaire described above, from 285 children aged five to twelve years, at the Fairburn Elementary School in West Los Angeles. Although the content of the questionnaire remained the same in the latter testing environment, the children were tested in classroom groups numbering from twenty-five to thirty-five children. The data obtained from the other group of children referred to the University for the correction of movement problems were obtained as part of a more comprehensive evaluation program, and these children were tested individually.

While the number of normal children who were administered the test is not sufficient to claim that norms have been established, it is believed that their mean scores afford rough averages which will make future comparisons of atypical groups and individual children with perceptual-motor problems more enlightening and meaningful.

Specific procedures are contained in the following paragraphs and are organized as follows: (a) descriptions of subject populations, (b) test procedures utilized with each of the two populations, (c) an enumeration of the manner in which the data were analyzed.

Subject Population

The children found in the population of normal children live in the west central part of Los Angeles, and most are from upper income families (median income about $20,000 per year).

Approximately one-half of the children are of the Jewish religion, with the remainder Protestants and assorted religions.

The proximity of a large Mormon Tabernacle results in a larger percentage of Mormons in the school than would be usual. Only .5 percent of the children are Negro, while about 10 percent have come from broken homes. Many of the families work at the University of California at Los Angeles.*

The children within the population of children with motor problems were referred to the laboratory at UCLA for remediation from a number of sources, including the Department of Pediatrics at the UCLA Medical Center, private physicians, school psychologists, parents and classroom teachers. Previous research indicated that about 95 percent evidence neurological "soft-signs," and when their motor abilities are compared to those of normal populations of children they are significantly inferior in tests of balance, agility, ball-handling skills and in the perception of body parts and of the left-right dimensions of their bodies. These children range in age from four to twelve years and are worked with by twelve instructors, in groups of from two to five children; most of them are boys. The children in this group are not severely physically handicapped, nor do they exhibit profound emotional problems. They normally come to the University for two hours a week for special motor training, and their average length of attendance in the program is about one year. Further delineation of the mean improvement they evidence, as well as their initial status with regard to drawing and gross motor skill, is dealt with in Chapter III.

Test Procedures

The children within the normal population were administered the test in classroom groups. The tester was introduced by the teacher, and he informed the children that they were to be given a questionnaire which would determine "how they felt

* Although it is obvious that the so-called normal population is highly distinctive and not representative of a typical cross-section of elementary school children in the United States, this group was selected because of the marked similarity between their economic level and that of the group of children coming to UCLA for remediation.

about themselves." It was explained that each question would be read and then they should indicate their first reaction to it by circling the "yes" or "no" at the end of the question. A request was made for questions, and the most common ones were "What is this for?" (answer: "For research at UCLA.") and "Will my teacher see this?" (generally asked by the older children and responded to negatively by the examiner).

Following the answering of questions, the questionnaires were passed out, face down, on each desk. The examiner then said, "Ready, turn them over," and when this was accomplished he then said, "The first question is," and read the question. After the question was read the examiner said, "Now circle "yes" or "no." Each question was read twice in this manner. This procedure continued until the entire questionnaire was read. "Forced answers" were requested, as the usual question to arise during the testing period was, "What if I can't decide?" The response of the tester was, "You must circle "yes" or "no." The testing, in each class, usually lasted for fifteen to twenty minutes.

Following this the questionnaires were collected after each child was asked to place his name and grade on the bottom, the teacher and children were thanked and the examiner left.

The children in the "motor problem" group were tested individually and were accorded the same instructions as outlined above. Their testing, however, was done on a one-to-one basis and was followed by and preceded by other tests in a more comprehensive test battery. Also, to gain rapport with the subjects the tester would often ask the child something about his family, his hobbies, etc.

Analysis of the Data

1. Preliminary analysis of the data included a visual survey of the questionnaires to determine whether they had been properly marked.

2. A total self-concept score was computed by adding together the responses on each questionnaire which were indicative of positive feelings. The range possible was thus 0 to 20. These total self-concept scores were analyzed by sex and by age within each of the two populations, and a comparison between populations was carried out.

3. Analysis of the questions was carried out and it was determined that each one was classifiable into five categories, including those indicative of feelings about general well-being, social competence, physical ability, physical appearance and school achievement. Two of these categories were divided into two parts each. The questions reflecting feelings about physical ability were divided into those indicative of ability in gross skills and questions about manipulative skills. The questions reflecting social competence were similarly divided into those dealing with general social ability and success and those involving social variables related to game participation. These categories and subcategories are contained in the section which follows, which outlines the findings, and are analyzed further throughout the remainder of the chapter.

4. An item analysis was carried out using the normal subjects. This was accomplished by analyzing whether each of the questions discriminated significantly between normal children who scored high (above the mean) and those who scored low (below the mean) in the total self-concept score obtained. This analysis was also carried out within each of the five categories and two subcategories enumerated in paragraph No. 3 above. Recommendations for refinement of the testing instrument were carried out following this analysis.

5. Age trends were computed by summarizing percent of positive answers for each question among the normal and "motor problem" groups. Analysis of total mean scores, by age, were also computed using the overall self-concept score, within the normal population.*

6. Sex differences in responses to individual questions and in mean self-concept scores were also contrasted within the normal population, as well as within the motor problem group. Intergroup comparisons, by sex, were also made when appropriate, contrasting the percent of positive response by question

---

* Throughout the study, when age trends were analyzed and when the responses of age variants were computed, the children were grouped into four groups: the five to six-year-olds, six and seven years, eight and nine years, nine and ten years, and eleven and twelve-year-olds. This was carried out because of the few number of subjects within a single age group.

and the total self-concept scores obtained from the normal and motor problem populations.

7. Selected questions were analyzed to determine the significance of various differences in percent of total responses elicited from normals versus children with motor problems, from boys versus girls, and from children within various age groups.

The findings were summarized and conclusions drawn relative to the use of the refinement of the self-concept questionnaire. These findings were utilized as a basis of the discussion found in the final part of this chapter.

FINDINGS

The findings are organized into two main divisions. The first part deals with analyses of the data collected from 285 normal children ranging in age from five to twelve years. The second section presents the findings emanating from a comparison of two groups of 133 boys and girls; one of these is considered a normal or average population, the second a population composed of children referred to the Perceptual-Motor Learning Laboratory at UCLA for evaluation and remediation of perceptual-motor difficulties.

Within the initial section the scores of the normal children are first analyzed by age and by sex. In addition, an item analysis is presented at the first part of this section in order to determine the internal validity of individual test items. When appropriate throughout the findings, the total questionnaire items are discussed within five subdivisions:

1. Questions reflecting general feelings the children expressed about themselves and their emotional state:

No. 9.   Do you wish you were different?

No. 10.   Are you sad most of the time?

No. 17.   Are you happy most of the time?

2. Questions dealing with general social competencies and social interactions in games, such as:

General social competency and interactions

No. 5.   Do your friends make fun of you?

No. 7.   Do you have trouble making friends?

No. 12.   Do girls like you?

No. 16.   Do boys like you?
No. 19.   Do you play with younger children a lot?
Social interaction in games
No. 11.   Are you the last to be chosen in games?
No. 13.   Are you a good leader in sports and games?
No. 15.   In games, do you watch instead of play?
3.   **Feelings about competencies in physical activity**
. . . *in gross motor activity*
No.   3.   Are you strong?
No. 14.   Are you clumsy?
. . . *in fine motor activity*
No.   1.   Are you good at making things with your hands?
No.   2.   Can you draw well?
4.   **Feelings about physical appearance**
No.   4.   Do you like the way you look?
No.   6.   Are you handsome/pretty?
No. 18.   Do you have nice hair?
5.   **Feelings about school and academic achievement**
No.   8.   Do you like school?
No. 20.   Is reading easy for you?

Development and Analysis of the Testing Instrument

The questions for the testing instrument used were originally gleaned by Piers and Harris from a list of Jersild's collection of statements about what children liked and disliked about themselves. Jersild's original list was grouped into several categories, including (a) physical characteristics and appearance, (b) clothing and grooming, (c) health and physical soundness, (d) home and family, (e) enjoyment of recreation, (f) ability in sports and play, (g) ability in school, attitudes toward school, (h) intellectual abilities, (i) special talents (i.e. music and arts), (j) just me, myself and (k) personality, character, inner resources, emotional tendencies (18, 23).

A preliminary pool of 164 statements within these categories was administered to ninety children from third, fourth and sixth grade classes by Piers and Harris, with the items being read aloud by the examiners. From this initial pilot study one hundred items were retained on the scale, which seemed to discriminate between children with high and low self-concepts.

In 1967, when searching for a self-concept test for children in our laboratory, the one hundred items isolated by Piers and Harris were inspected by Mr. Tom Durkin, who was working on a more global test battery, and together with other researchers in the laboratory, the twenty questions used in this investigation were selected. This was done to shorten administration time, permitting more time for tests of motor ability, game choice and the like. Piers and Harris found that their one hundred items were internally consistent and reasonably reliable for a test of this type (test-retest r's = .71 to .72), with a four-month period separating the testing periods. We have found similar reliabilities when test-retest comparison of the scores obtained from the twenty-item test we have used had been contrasted. Higher correlations were obtained (i.e., r = .82) when the test-retest periods were separated by one week.

Following the testing of the normal children in this investigation from ages five to twelve, as described in the previous section (Procedures), their questionnaires were inspected to determine whether instructions had been followed. It was found that 45 percent of the questionnaires obtained from the five-year-old children had to be discarded due to the fact that they had failed to mark all answers, had answered both "yes" and "no" to the same question or had otherwise failed to follow instructions. Twenty percent of the questionnaires obtained from the six-year-olds in the population were discarded as invalid for similar reasons, while none of the questionnaires obtained from the seven-year-olds and older were marked incorrectly.

The findings relative to age differences in the scores reported later must therefore be interpreted with this in mind. The scores from the five and six-year-olds utilized in the study are therefore probably from children who are more intelligent and more capable of understanding and following verbal directions.

Following this initial survey of the questionnaires, each was scored relative to the number of answers out of twenty which indicated a positive self-concept on the part of the child. Thus a score of 20 was indicative of a high self-concept, while 5 was indicative of a low self-concept. The mean score obtained from 288 children of both sexes from the ages of five to twelve was 15.1, with a standard deviation of 3.21.

TABLE I

MEAN SCORES OF SELF-CONCEPT TEST BY AGE AND SEX
OF THE 288 NORMAL CHILDREN

	Boys				Total Boys	Girls				Total Girls	Total Subjects
Age	5-6	7-8	9-10	11-12		5-6	7-8	9-10	11-12		
Number	22	70	44	11	147	27	60	45	9	141	288
Mean	14.5	15.4	15.6	15.7	15.3	14.1	15.1	14.9	14.4	14.8	15.1
S.D.	2.86	3.19	2.62	3.33	3.15	3.00	3.62	2.69	3.95	3.29	3.21

Using the total self-concept scores, one-way analyses of variance were computed to determine if there were any significant age differences. There was found to be no significant difference between the total mean scores from the girls and those obtained from the boys (t = .25). Similarly, no significant age trends were revealed in the analyses of variance. (F scores, when the boys' scores by age were compared, was 1.19; and F = .45 when the girls' scores by age were contrasted.) As can be seen in Table I, scores of the adjacent age groups (i.e. 5 and 6-year-olds) have been combined to make more valid comparisons between age groups, due to the few number of subjects within the single age groups.

The mean age for the total boys' population was 8.21 (S.D. 1.63) while the mean age of the girls was 8.11 (S.D. 1.52). The age and standard deviation for the total population was 8.17 (S.D. 1.88).

Item Analysis

To further examine the validity of the questionnaire, an item analysis was undertaken contrasting the percentages of "yes" responses on each question on the part of children scoring above the mean in the self-concept test and those scoring below the mean. The scores of the boys and girls having a mean self-concept score of 15 were discarded (N=23 omitted), and thus the high self-concept children had scores of 16 or higher, while those of the low self-concept group had scores of 14 or lower.

As can be seen, significantly more of the boys, as might be the percentages of the high and low self-concept groups resulted in significant differences (at the 5% level) between the two groups in the expected directions. For example, only 8 percent of the high self-concept group stated that they watched instead of played games, while 37 percent of the low self-concept group answered this question with a "yes."

TABLE II

COMPARISON OF PERCENTAGES OF "YES" RESPONSES TO QUESTIONS BY 165 CHILDREN SCORING HIGH IN THE TOTAL SELF-CONCEPT SCORE, TO RESPONSES OF 111 CHILDREN SCORING LOW IN THE SELF-CONCEPT SCORE

	High Self-Concept Group $N = 165$	Low Self-Concept Group $N = 111$	Difference	t
	%	%	%	
1. Are you good at making things with you hands?	92	73	19	3.87*
2. Can you draw well?	79	67	12	2.11*
3. Are you strong?	86	57	29	5.09*
4. Do you like the way you look?	88	46	42	7.50*
5. Do your friends make fun of you?	17	55	38	6.55*
6. Are you handsome/pretty?	88	64	24	4.44*
7. Do you have trouble making friends?	13	49	36	6.32*
8. Do you like school?	82	60	22	3.86*
9. Do you wish you were different?	18	63	45	7.89*
10. Are you sad most of the time?	05	35	30	5.66*
11. Are you the last to be chosen in games?	22	56	34	5.76*
12. Do girls like you?	76	60	16	2.71*
13. Are you a good leader in games and sports?	87	57	30	5.36*
14. Are you clumsy?	08	40	32	6.04*
15. In games do you watch instead of play?	08	37	29	5.58*
16. Do boys like you?	79	49	30	5.08*
17. Are you happy most of the time?	98	74	24	5.22*
18. Do you have nice hair?	93	67	26	5.09*
19. Do you play with younger children a lot?	42	59	17	2.75*
20. Is reading easy for you?	92	78	14	3.04*

* Differences significant at 5 percent level.

Similarly, when the low self-concept children were asked if they believed themselves clumsy, 40 percent answered in the affirmative, while only 8 percent of the children having a high overall self-concept perceived themselves physically inept.

Overall, it appears that children having generally negative feelings about themselves do not feel that they can make things well with their hands, that they are not strong and do not like the way they look. It appears that the same children have trouble in peer relationships, and about half of these children reported trouble making friends, that they are chosen last in games and are not liked by either boys or girls. Furthermore, about one-third of this group reported that they are unhappy most of the time (and are sad most of the time), they do not like school, they wish they were different, they do not consider themselves physically attractive (handsome/or pretty), and they play with younger children "a lot."

The responses of the group high in the total self-concept scores are in marked contrast to the scores outlined in the previous paragraph. Most of these children feel themselves good at making things with their hands, that they are strong and that they are good leaders in sports and games. Similarly, their social relationships appear reasonably happy, as they state that they seldom watch, but instead play, have little trouble making friends and are liked by both boys and girls. They report being happy most of the time, are seldom sad, find reading easy and generally enjoy school.

Sex Differences

As was stated, no significant sex differences were found when the total self-concept scores of the normal girls were contrasted to those of the normal boys ($t = .25$). It was, however, believed helpful to further analyze the responses to individual questions answered by the girls and the boys. The results of this analysis may be seen in Graph I as well as in Table III. The latter contains t-scores computed on percentages which appeared significantly different.

As can be seen in Table II, in all cases the comparison of expected, reported themselves as strong; more of the girls reported playing with younger children and liking school. The boys reported being liked by boys, while the girls reported being liked by their feminine companions. The general hostility (feigned or real) usually seen in elementary school between boys and girls was also reflected in these responses, which suggested that both boys and girls perceived the children of the opposite sex as not liking them.

TABLE III

COMPARISON OF PERCENT OF "YES" RESPONSES TO QUESTIONNAIRE
ITEMS BY THE NORMAL GIRLS TO THOSE OF THE NORMAL BOYS

Question	Total Subjects $N=285$	Girls $N=149$	Boys $N=136$	Diff.	t
	%	%	%	%	
1. Are you good at making things with your hands?	85	84	86	02	.30
2. Can you draw well?	76	79	74	05	.81
3. Are you strong?	72	62	82	20	3.85*
4. Do you like the way you look?	72	67	77	10	1.85
5. Do your friends make fun of you?	32	32	32	00	00
6. Are you handsome/pretty?	78	77	80	03	.40
7. Do you have trouble making friends?	27	28	26	02	.3
8. Do you like school?	74	79	68	11	2.12*
9. Do you wish you were different?	36	39	33	06	1.05
10. Are you sad most of the time?	16	18	13	05	1.19
11. Are you the last to be chosen in games?	34	36	32	04	.56
12. Do girls like you?	*	89	50	39	7.80*
13. Are you a good leader in games and sports	75	74	76	02	.30
14. Are you clumsy?	16	19	17	02	.30
15. In games, do you watch instead of play?	21	21	21	00	00
16. Do boys like you?	*	46	95	49	10.89*
17. Are you happy most of the time?	90	86	93	07	1.94
18. Do you have nice hair?	83	81	85	04	.41
19. Do you play with younger children a lot?	49	60	37	23	3.97*
20. Is reading easy for you?	83	87	77	10	2.17*

* Differences significant at 5 percent level.

Age Differences

Although the previous reviewed analysis of variance did not reveal any significant age trends (within either sex) when the total self-concept scores were compared, it was felt helpful to compare the percentage of "yes" responses to the various questions by children within the various age groups. The results of that analysis may be found in Graphs II and III.

Inspection of these graphs reveals that, in general, as children mature they express more positive self-concepts about their participation in group games and in peer relationships. More of the younger boys, for example, reported watching instead of playing, and the younger boys reported having more trouble making friends than did the older boys. It must be remembered that the reports from the five and six-year-olds pictures on these graphs were from only 55 percent of the total population of five and six-year-olds to whom these questionnaires were administered. Thus, conceivably, the responses from the less able children of this age group would have reflected even more marked problems of this nature. It should be similarly noted that more of the younger boys reported feeling themselves "clumsy" than was reflected in the self-reports of the older males.

Responses of both the younger boys and younger girls reflected the feeling that a larger percent of them are sad most of the time than was found in the responses of the older children. Younger girls reported watching instead of playing games, and there seems to be a regular drop-off of this response by age (Graph III). This same trend is seen in the boys' responses (Graph II). Both groups of nine and ten-year-old boys and girls reported more often that they perceive being disliked by the opposite sex than is reported by the younger and older age groups surveyed.

Comparison of Self-Concept Scores of Normal Children to Those Obtained from Children Evidencing Perceptual-Motor Deficiencies

In order to determine whether measurable perceptual-motor deficiencies are associated with measures of expressed feelings related to the self-concept, a matched group of normal children within the previous population surveyed in Part I were compared to an equal number (133) of children who had been evaluated at the Perceptual-Motor Learning Laboratory at UCLA. This latter group evidenced significant differences in a six-category test of gross motor ability problems including difficulty in drawing and the like. The physical characteristic most likely to distinguish them as a group from normal children is found in the scores obtained from tests of balance (33).

The children in the two groups were matched by age and sex as follows: 22 girls—4 in each group were five to six years of age, 7 were seven to eight years of age, 8 were nine to ten years of

GRAPH I

PERCENTAGE OF BOYS AND GIRLS ANSWERING "YES" TO EACH QUESTION

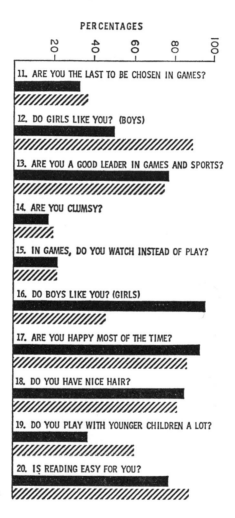

PERCENTAGES

11. ARE YOU THE LAST TO BE CHOSEN IN GAMES?

12. DO GIRLS LIKE YOU? (BOYS)

13. ARE YOU A GOOD LEADER IN GAMES AND SPORTS?

14. ARE YOU CLUMSY?

15. IN GAMES, DO YOU WATCH INSTEAD OF PLAY?

16. DO BOYS LIKE YOU? (GIRLS)

17. ARE YOU HAPPY MOST OF THE TIME?

18. DO YOU HAVE NICE HAIR?

19. DO YOU PLAY WITH YOUNGER CHILDREN A LOT?

20. IS READING EASY FOR YOU?

GRAPH II

PERCENTAGE OF NORMAL BOYS FROM FOUR AGE GROUPS
ANSWERING "YES" TO EACH QUESTION

PERCENTAGES

20 40 60 80 100

1. ARE YOU GOOD AT MAKING THINGS WITH YOUR HANDS?

2. CAN YOU DRAW WELL?

3. ARE YOU STRONG?

4. DO YOU LIKE THE WAY YOU LOOK?

5. DO YOUR FRIENDS MAKE FUN OF YOU?

6. ARE YOU HANDSOME / PRETTY?

7. DO YOU HAVE TROUBLE MAKING FRIENDS?

8. DO YOU LIKE SCHOOL?

9. DO YOU WISH YOU WERE DIFFERENT?

10. ARE YOU SAD MOST OF THE TIME?

5-6 YEARS (N=22)

7-8 YEARS (N=70)

9-10 YEARS (N=44)

11-12 YEARS (N=11)

PERCENTAGES

20   40   60   80   100

11. ARE YOU THE LAST TO BE CHOSEN IN GAMES?

12. DO GIRLS LIKE YOU?

13. ARE YOU A GOOD LEADER IN GAMES AND SPORTS?

14. ARE YOU CLUMSY?

15. IN GAMES, DO YOU WATCH INSTEAD OF PLAY?

16. DO BOYS LIKE YOU?

17. ARE YOU HAPPY MOST OF THE TIME?

18. DO YOU HAVE NICE HAIR?

19. DO YOU PLAY WITH YOUNGER CHILDREN A LOT?

20. IS READING EASY FOR YOU?

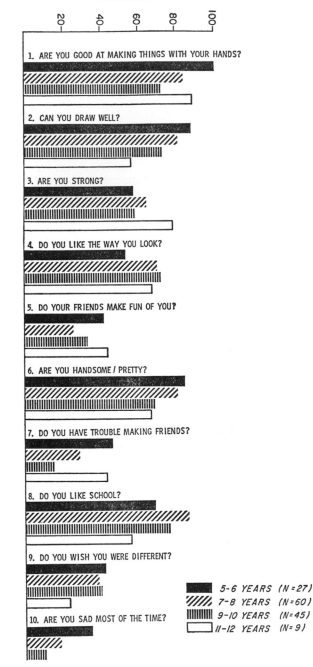

GRAPH III

PERCENTAGE OF NORMAL GIRLS FROM FOUR AGE GROUPS
ANSWERING "YES" TO EACH QUESTION

PERCENTAGES

1. ARE YOU GOOD AT MAKING THINGS WITH YOUR HANDS?

2. CAN YOU DRAW WELL?

3. ARE YOU STRONG?

4. DO YOU LIKE THE WAY YOU LOOK?

5. DO YOUR FRIENDS MAKE FUN OF YOU?

6. ARE YOU HANDSOME / PRETTY?

7. DO YOU HAVE TROUBLE MAKING FRIENDS?

8. DO YOU LIKE SCHOOL?

9. DO YOU WISH YOU WERE DIFFERENT?

10. ARE YOU SAD MOST OF THE TIME?

5-6 YEARS (N = 27)
7-8 YEARS (N = 60)
9-10 YEARS (N = 45)
11-12 YEARS (N = 9)

20 40 60 80 100

11. ARE YOU THE LAST TO BE CHOSEN IN GAMES?

12. DO GIRLS LIKE YOU?

13. ARE YOU A GOOD LEADER IN GAMES AND SPORTS?

14. ARE YOU CLUMSY?

15. IN GAMES, DO YOU WATCH INSTEAD OF PLAY?

16. DO BOYS LIKE YOU?

17. ARE YOU HAPPY MOST OF THE TIME?

18. DO YOU HAVE NICE HAIR?

19. DO YOU PLAY WITH YOUNGER CHILDREN A LOT?

20. IS READING EASY FOR YOU?

age, and 3 were eleven to twelve years of age. The 111 boys' scores used for comparative purposes in the investigation ranged as follows: 22 were five to six years of age, 45 were seven to eight years, 33 were nine to ten years, and 11 were eleven to twelve years of age.

When their total self-concept scores were compared, based upon answers indicative of a positive self-concept, it was found that (Table IV) significant differences occurred between the boys' scores, but not when those of the girls in the two groups were contrasted (t's equalled 2.78 and 1.13 respectively).

TABLE IV

COMPARISON OF TOTAL MEAN SELF-CONCEPT SCORES BY SEX, BY CHILDREN IDENTIFIED AS HAVING MOVEMENT PROBLEMS TO CHILDREN FROM A NORMAL POPULATION

	Normal Boys	Movement Problem Boys	Normal Girls	Movement Problem Girls
N	111	111	22	22
M	15.23	14.00	14.36	13.54
S.D.	3.271	3.315	2.996	3.578
S.E.	.311	.316	.652	.779
t		2.777		1.13

Although the mean scores of the two girl's groups are different in the expected direction, it is possible that with additional subjects significant differences would have been obtained. At the same time it is equally possible that due to the difference in cultural emphasis upon physical ability of girls, differences in a total score from the self-concept test employed in this investigation would not appear when the scores of "clumsy" girls are contrasted to those of normal girls. Physical ability may not contribute as much to a girl's feelings about herself as it does to a boy's self-concept.

It is also true that the physical attributes of the "normal" population employed in this investigation were not surveyed. Thus it is highly probable that from 5 to 15 percent of this group were children who would evidence measurable coordination problems had they been evaluated. Had the children with motor problems been screened from the normal children it is probable that the differences in self-concept would have been more distinct than is indicated by the statistics presented in Table IV.

Analysis by Question

In an effort to illuminate possible differences in the self-concept of children with movement problems when contrasted to normal children, analyses of the percent of "yes" responses to the various questions were carried out and are found in Tables V and VI. To determine the significance of the various percentages arrived at, "t" scores were computed, as shown.

TABLE V

COMPARISONS OF THE PERCENT OF "YES" RESPONSES, BY QUESTION, OBTAINED FROM NORMAL BOYS TO PERCENT OF "YES" RESPONSES OBTAINED FROM BOYS WITH MOVEMENT PROBLEMS

Question	Normal Boys $N = 111$	Movement Problem Boys $N = 111$	Difference	t
	%	%	%	
1. Are you good at making things with your hands?	87	78	9	1.80
2. Can you draw well?	76	66	10	1.67
3. Are you strong?	90	80	10	2.13*
4. Do you like the way you look?	77	76	1	.18
5. Do your friends make fun of you?	34	57	23	3.38*
6. Are you handsome/pretty?	81	77	4	.73
7. Do you have trouble making friends?	27	40	13	2.06
8. Do you like school?	67	77	10	1.67
9. Do you wish you were different?	33	36	3	.46
10. Are you sad most of the time?	14	27	13	2.64*
11. Are you the last to be chosen in games?	34	42	8	1.23
12. Do girls like you?	53	50	3	.45
13. Are you a good leader in games and sports?	19	26	7	1.43
14. Are you clumsy?	19	26	7	1.43
15. In games, do you watch instead of play?	23	35	12	2.03*
16. Do boys like you?	87	87	00	.00
17. Are you happy most of the time?	91	90	1	.26
18. Do you have nice hair?	84	83	1	.20
19. Do you play with younger children a lot?	37	40	13	1.94
20. Is reading easy for you?	85	60	25	4.39*

* Differences significant at 5 percent level.

These same differences are contrasted in Graphs III and IV. As can be seen, the percentages of "yes" responses in the questions dealing with strength, friendships, whether the child felt sad and whether he watched or played in games, revealed significant differences between the two groups. More of the normal boys (85%) reported that reading was easy for them, as contrasted to the children with movement problems (60%). In general, the responses from the two groups revealed that 40 percent of the boys with movement problems reported having difficulty making friends, while 57 percent of these same boys reported that their friends made fun of them. In contrast, only 27 percent of the boys from the normal population reported that they had trouble making friends, while only 34 percent reported that their friends made fun of them.

Although no significant differences were obtained in the percentages of positive responses elicited in the contrasted groups of girls (perhaps because of the small number involved), there were interesting differences obtained (Table VI). Three times as many girls with movement problems reported that they are clumsy, while twice as many of this same group reported that they had trouble making friends, as was reported by the girls matched from the normal group. Only 14 percent of the girls from the normal population reported that they were not good at making things with their hands, while 36 percent of the girls in the contrasted group gave negative answers to this same question.

The girls with motor problems thus seemed more likely to give answers indicative of a negative self-concept to questions dealing directly with physical activity. On the other hand, the boys with movement problems gave negative answers which reflected concerns about social relationships with their peers.

Age Differences in Scores of Boys Evidencing Movement Problems

Scores of the girls at various ages were not surveyed, as the number of girls (22) was considered inadequate for any valid comparisons. On the other hand, the survey of the scores of the "movement problem" boys on the previous page reveals

TABLE VI

COMPARISONS OF THE PERCENT OF "YES" RESPONSES, BY QUESTION
OBTAINED FROM NORMAL GIRLS TO PERCENT OF "YES"
RESPONSES OBTAINED FROM GIRLS WITH
MOVEMENT PROBLEMS

Questions	Normal Girls N = 22	Movement Problem Girls N = 22	Difference	t
	%	%	%	
1. Are you good at making things with your hands?	86	64	22	1.80
2. Can you draw well?	82	77	5	.42
3. Are you strong?	55	64	9	.63
4. Do you like the way you look?	73	82	9	.76
5. Do your friends make fun of you?	36	64	28	1.99
6. Are you handsome/pretty?	77	77	0	.00
7. Do you have trouble making friends?	23	50	27	1.97
8. Do you like school?	86	91	5	.56
9. Do you wish you were different?	36	55	19	1.32
10. Are you sad most of the time?	19	27	8	.68
11. Are you the last to be chosen in games?	45	64	19	1.32
12. Do girls like you?	95	82	13	1.46
13. Are you a good leader in games and sports?	73	59	14	1.04
14. Are you clumsy?	09	27	16	1.54
15. In games, do you watch instead of play?	32	32	0	.00
16. Do boys like you?	41	55	14	.97
17. Are you happy most of the time?	91	82	9	.96
18. Do you have nice hair?	95	77	8	.80
19. Do you play with younger children a lot?	77	55	22	1.61
20. Is reading easy for you?	91	91	0	.00

several interesting trends. It appears, for example, that the boys are less likely to report their friends making fun of them as they grow older. Whether they begin to incur less peer punishment or whether they become increasingly hesitant to report it in the direct way required by the questionnaire is, of course, difficult to determine. Similarly, the boys with motor problems are less likely to perceive themselves as "good leaders" in sports and in games as they grow older.

It is difficult to judge whether the marked differences in the scores elicited from the five to six-year-old group, when contrasted to the reports of the adjacent age group, on several of

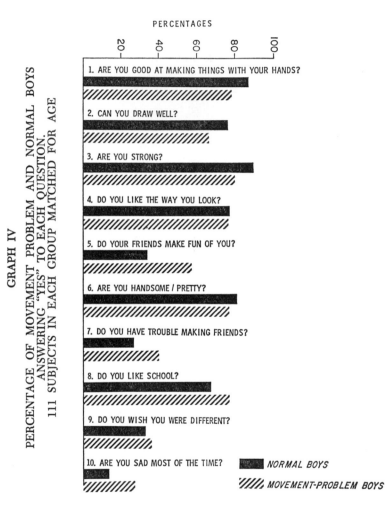

PERCENTAGES

GRAPH IV

PERCENTAGE OF MOVEMENT PROBLEM AND NORMAL BOYS
ANSWERING "YES" TO EACH QUESTION.
111 SUBJECTS IN EACH GROUP MATCHED FOR AGE

1. ARE YOU GOOD AT MAKING THINGS WITH YOUR HANDS?

2. CAN YOU DRAW WELL?

3. ARE YOU STRONG?

4. DO YOU LIKE THE WAY YOU LOOK?

5. DO YOUR FRIENDS MAKE FUN OF YOU?

6. ARE YOU HANDSOME / PRETTY?

7. DO YOU HAVE TROUBLE MAKING FRIENDS?

8. DO YOU LIKE SCHOOL?

9. DO YOU WISH YOU WERE DIFFERENT?

10. ARE YOU SAD MOST OF THE TIME?

NORMAL BOYS

MOVEMENT-PROBLEM BOYS

PERCENTAGES

11. ARE YOU THE LAST TO BE CHOSEN IN GAMES?

12. DO GIRLS LIKE YOU?

13. ARE YOU A GOOD LEADER IN GAMES AND SPORTS?

14. ARE YOU CLUMSY?

15. IN GAMES, DO YOU WATCH INSTEAD OF PLAY?

16. DO BOYS LIKE YOU?

17. ARE YOU HAPPY MOST OF THE TIME?

18. DO YOU HAVE NICE HAIR?

19. DO YOU PLAY WITH YOUNGER CHILDREN A LOT?

20. IS READING EASY FOR YOU?

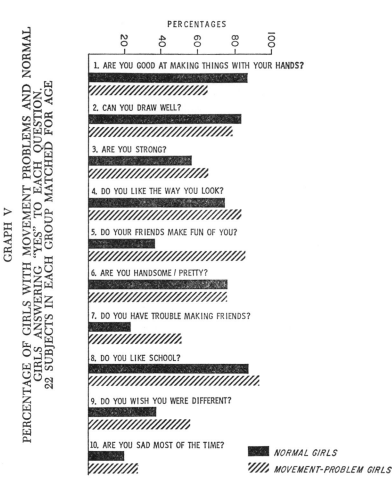

GRAPH V

PERCENTAGE OF GIRLS WITH MOVEMENT PROBLEMS AND NORMAL GIRLS ANSWERING "YES" TO EACH QUESTION. 22 SUBJECTS IN EACH GROUP MATCHED FOR AGE

PERCENTAGES

20   40   60   80   100

1. ARE YOU GOOD AT MAKING THINGS WITH YOUR HANDS?

2. CAN YOU DRAW WELL?

3. ARE YOU STRONG?

4. DO YOU LIKE THE WAY YOU LOOK?

5. DO YOUR FRIENDS MAKE FUN OF YOU?

6. ARE YOU HANDSOME / PRETTY?

7. DO YOU HAVE TROUBLE MAKING FRIENDS?

8. DO YOU LIKE SCHOOL?

9. DO YOU WISH YOU WERE DIFFERENT?

10. ARE YOU SAD MOST OF THE TIME?

NORMAL GIRLS

MOVEMENT-PROBLEM GIRLS

PERCENTAGES

11. ARE YOU THE LAST TO BE CHOSEN IN GAMES?

12. DO GIRLS LIKE YOU?

13. ARE YOU A GOOD LEADER IN GAMES AND SPORTS?

14. ARE YOU CLUMSY?

15. IN GAMES DO YOU WATCH INSTEAD OF PLAY?

16. DO BOYS LIKE YOU?

17. ARE YOU HAPPY MOST OF THE TIME?

18. DO YOU HAVE NICE HAIR?

19. DO YOU PLAY WITH YOUNGER CHILDREN A LOT?

20. IS READING EASY FOR YOU?

GRAPH VI

PERCENTAGE OF MOVEMENT PROBLEM BOYS FROM FOUR AGE
GROUPS ANSWERING "YES" TO EACH QUESTION

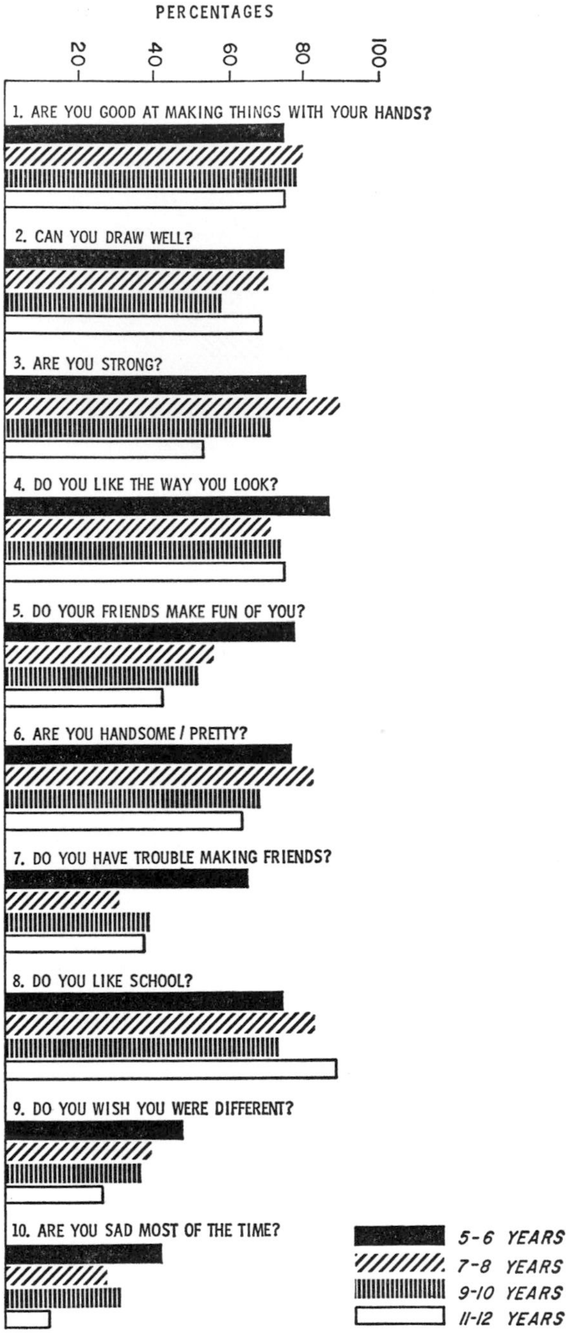

PERCENTAGES

1. ARE YOU GOOD AT MAKING THINGS WITH YOUR HANDS?

2. CAN YOU DRAW WELL?

3. ARE YOU STRONG?

4. DO YOU LIKE THE WAY YOU LOOK?

5. DO YOUR FRIENDS MAKE FUN OF YOU?

6. ARE YOU HANDSOME / PRETTY?

7. DO YOU HAVE TROUBLE MAKING FRIENDS?

8. DO YOU LIKE SCHOOL?

9. DO YOU WISH YOU WERE DIFFERENT?

10. ARE YOU SAD MOST OF THE TIME?

5-6 YEARS
7-8 YEARS
9-10 YEARS
11-12 YEARS

20 40 60 80 100

11. ARE YOU THE LAST TO BE CHOSEN IN GAMES?

12. DO GIRLS LIKE YOU?

13. ARE YOU A GOOD LEADER IN GAMES AND SPORTS?

14. ARE YOU CLUMSY?

15. IN GAMES DO YOU WATCH INSTEAD OF PLAY?

16. DO BOYS LIKE YOU?

17. ARE YOU HAPPY MOST OF THE TIME?

18. DO YOU HAVE NICE HAIR?

19. DO YOU PLAY WITH YOUNGER CHILDREN A LOT?

20. IS READING EASY FOR YOU?

the questions (i.e. Nos. 11 and 14) are due to the fact that the younger children had a more difficult time understanding the questions or whether real shifts in a child's feelings of rejection in physical performance situations is initially felt between the ages of five to eight years. It is believed that the latter hypothesis is the more tenable one.

Summary of the Findings

1. The questionnaire was found to be appropriate for group administration only for normal children of seven years of age or above.

2. All twenty of the questionnaire items were valid and differentiated significantly between children with low and high self-concepts, obtained from a total score on the same test.

3. The total concept score of normal children, based upon a 0 to 20 point scale, was 15.07, with a standard deviation of 3.22.

4. There were no significant age trends nor sex differences in the means of the total self-concept scores obtained.

5. Sex differences in responses to questions analyzed separately indicated that girls reported playing with younger children more than did boys, and girls said that they liked school more often than did boys.

6. Boys responded positively to the question concerning physical strength more frequently than did the girls in the normal population.

7. Age trends surveyed among the normal population, based upon responses to individual questions, revealed that the younger boys were more likely to express negative feelings about peer relations in games than were older boys, and that the younger girls expressed similar feelings (i.e. "they would rather watch than play").

8. Between the ages of nine and ten, according to these data, both boys and girls were more likely to report being disliked by the opposite sex than was true when the responses of children within the younger or older age groups were surveyed.

9. The results of the portion of the study in which responses of the self-concept test obtained from a matched group of 133 normal children and 133 children with motor problems revealed

significant differences in the mean scores obtained between the respective boys' groups, but not when the girls' groups were compared.

10. The girls evidencing movement problems were more likely to express negative self-concepts about specific movement attributes ("strength," "making things with their hands" and "being clumsy"); on the other hand, the boys in the same group were more likely to express negative feelings about peer relationships than about movement competencies.

SUMMARY, CONCLUSIONS AND IMPLICATIONS

The two-part investigation had as its aim the analysis of a short form of a test of self-concept for use with children. Secondly, it was purposed to compare the responses given to the questionnaire items by normal children to those obtained from children with perceptual-motor problems. Following an analysis of the form utilized, it was concluded that it was a helpful and reliable measure of self-concept in children which could be administered to groups of children with normal intellects above the age of seven years. An item analysis indicated that all of the questionnaires significantly discriminated between children with low versus high self-concepts based upon their total scores on the questionnaires. No significant sex or age trends were noted in this analysis.

The comparison of responses between children with motor problems and those from a normal population showed that the boys' responses indicated that those possessing motor deficiencies expressed significantly more problems when dealing with social situations connected with games, while the comparison of the female responses indicated that the girls with motor problems were likely to make direct reference to perceived ineptitude in physical tasks.

The obvious objection to such a study, of course, is whether a questionnaire of this nature obtains "true" measures of the child's feelings about himself. The investigators were left with this same question after observing the attitudes of some of the older children when taking the questionnaire and those of the younger ones who apparently failed to understand some of the questions, particularly the five and six-year-old children. At the same time, it is believed that when the responses of the child or group of children are considered, using such a questionnaire, rough guidelines for possible future psychological counseling are provided. For example, if a child expresses more than eight or nine answers reflecting negative feelings about himself, which would place him within the lower 15 percent of the test's norm, it is likely that he is suffering from feelings with which he needs help, or at least that he needs a more thorough psychological "work-up."

In modern society, however, many children become extremely "test wise" and thus can easily "fake" either negative or positive answers to any of the questions, if they desire. We became aware, when giving the questionnaire to innumerable children with perceptual-motor problems, that the more stable of these children would readily admit to experiencing difficulties connected with their performance of games and physical skills. On the other hand, children who were apparently suffering from more extensive emotional problems would sometimes conceal their problems from relatively unsophisticated "probings" of the questionnaire.

It is believed that several points are interesting to note upon surveying the data collected in this study. For example, it is interesting to be able to objectify the apparent hostility that children in middle childhood frequently express about the opposite sex. The responses of the nine and ten-year-olds to questions about being liked by boys and girls confirmed this frequently heard childhood assertion.

It was also interesting to note the oblique manner in which the boys with motor problems apparently dealt with the questions such as "Are you clumsy?" and the like. They tended to mention their difficulties within the social context rather than to affirm what was corroborated by the motor performance tests—that they were indeed clumsy. Several possibilities, of course, are suggested by this evasiveness on their part: (a) they are consciously avoiding telling someone how they feel about themselves physically, (b) they do not know how poorly they perform in motor skills and/or (c) they are engaging in some kind of extrapunitive aggression against their peers for their rejection in games rather than attributing their lack of acceptance to personal inadequacies, i.e. their lack of physical skills that make them helpful to childhood teams.

The "motor problem" girls, on the other hand, seemed less reluctant to admit their inability to perform with their total body and with their hands, perhaps reflecting the general assumption that there is less social stigma placed upon physical ineptitude in girls and thus less anxiety accompanying the admission of "clumsiness" on the part of females.

The consistency of responses concerned with the manner in which the children felt about a wide range of social, personal and academic experiences suggests that future work should more thoroughly explore the mutual affectivity of a child's general feelings about his body, his performance, his school and his social competencies. Weatherford, among others, has begun to investigate these interesting relationships, and the data collected in this investigation suggest even more avenues of study (31).

Particularly intriguing, of course, are the findings from a previous study in which this same questionnaire was used prior to and after a group of children had registered significant improvement in physical skill (10). While skill improvement had taken place, the children had apparently not perceived or not believed that this improvement was important, for the same percentage of children continued to report themselves as "clumsy" and/or the last to be chosen in games. This latter finding suggests these hypotheses: (a) physical changes occur more rapidly than feelings about one's physique and physical capacities, (b) the responses to the questionnaire may become less guarded as the child begins to experience success and so he will admit to negative feelings more readily as he continues to be tested on successive days, or (c) physical skill and appearance are not as important in the formation of the child's total self-concept as is believed by many.

It is probable that children vary markedly concerning how much importance they attach to their physical prowess. A child's feelings of success and failure in a given area of competency are dictated by parental reactions* as well as by innumerable constitutional and environmental variables. Thus further studies might explore individual differences in value attached to physical ability in children as a function of how much their self-concept may be heightened via improvement in physical skill.

BIBLIOGRAPHY

1. ADAMS, N., AND CALDWELL, W.: The Children's Somatic Apperception Test. *J Gen Psychol, 68*:43-57, 1963.
2. BENTON, A. L.: *Right-Left Discrimination and Finger Localization.* New York, Hoeber, 1959.
3. BERGES, J., AND LEZINE, I.: *The Imitation of Gestures* (translated by Arthur Parmalee). London, The Spastics Society Medical Education and Information Unit in Association with Wm. Heinemann Medical Books, 1965.
4. CLIFTON, M. A., AND SMITH, HOPE M.: Viewing oneself performing selected motor skills in motion pictures and its effect upon the expressed consciousness of self in performance. *Res Quart Amer Ass Health Phys Educ, 33*:369-375, 1962.
5. COPPERSMITH, S.: A method for determining types of self-esteem. *J Abnorm Soc Psychol, 59*:87-94, 1959.
6. CRATTY, B. J.: *Perceptual-Motor Attributes of Retarded Children.* Monograph, Department of Physical Education, University of California, Los Angeles, 1966.
7. CRATTY, B. J.: *Social Dimensions of Physical Activity.* Englewood Cliffs, N. J., Prentice-Hall, 1967, Ch. 3.
8. CRATTY, B. J.: *Motor Activity and the Education of Retardates.* Philadelphia, Lea & F., 1969.
9. CRATTY, B. J.: *Perceptual and Motor Development in Infants and Children.* New York, Macmillan, 1970, Ch. IV.
10. CRATTY, B. J., AND MARTIN, M. M.: *Perceptual-Motor Attributes in Children.* Philadelphia, Lea & F., 1969.
11. CRATTY, B. J., AND SAMS, T. A.: *The Body Image of Blind Children.* The American Foundation for the Blind. A State of the Art Report for International Research Information Service, July, 1968.
12. CORWNE, D. D., AND STEPHENS, M. W.: Self-acceptance and self-evaluative behavior: a critique of methodology. *Psychol Bull, 58*:104-121, 1961.
13. FREUD, S.: In Brill, A. A. (Ed.): *The Basic Writings of Sigmund Freud.* New York, Modern Lib., 1938.

---

* Zeller, for example, has obtained .7 correlations between measures of parental attitudes about physical education and their children's physical performance scores (32).

14. GASSER, O. F.: Weight training and self-concept. M.A. Thesis, Department of Physical Education, University of California, Los Angeles, 1965.
15. GOTTESMAN, E., AND BROWN, L. W.: The body image identification test: a quantitative technique to study an aspect of the body image. *J Genet Psychol, 108*:19-34, 1966.
16. GORLOW, L.; BUTLER, A., AND GUTHERIE, G.: Correlates of self-attitudes of retardates. *Amer J Ment Defic, 67*:549-554, 1963.
17. INGLIS, J.: Abnormalities of motivation and "ego functions." In Eysenck, H. J. (Ed.): *Handbook of Abnormal Psychology*. New York, Basic Books, 1960.
18. JERSILD, A. T.: *In Search of Self*. New York, Teachers College Columbia University, Bureau of Publications, 1952.
19. KELLOGG, RHODA: Children's art as a mental test. In *Analyzing Children's Art*. Palo Alto, National Press Books, 1969.
20. LEIGHTON, J.; CUPP, M.; PRINCE, A.; PHILADAUM, D., AND McLARREN, M.: The effect of a physical fitness development program on self-concept, mental age and job proficiency in the mentally retarded. *J Phys Ment Rehab, 20*:4-11, 1966.
21. OLIVER, J. N.: The effect of physical conditioning exercises and activities on the mental characteristics of educationally sub-normal boys. *Brit J Educ Psychol, 28*:155-165, 1958.
22. PERKINS, H. V.: Factors influencing change in children's self-concept. *Child Develop, 29*:221-230, 1958.
23. PIERS, E. V., AND HARRIS, D. B.: Age and other correlates of self-concept in children. *J Educ Psychol, 55*:91-95, 1964.
24. READ, DONALD A.: The influence of competitive and non-competitive programs of physical education on body-image and self-concept. Paper presented at the National Convention, American Association of Health, Recreation and Physical Education, Boston, Mass., April 1969.
25. RODGERS, C., AND DYMOND, R.: *Psychotherapy and Personality Change*. Chicago, U. of Chicago, 1954.
26. SCHILDER, P.: *The Image and Appearance of the Human Body*. New York, Int. Univs., 1950.
27. SEARS, P.: Level of aspiration in relation to some variables of personality, clinical studies. *J Soc Psychol, 14*:311-336, 1941.
28. SECORD, P. F., AND JOURARD, S. M.: The appraisal of body-cathexis: body-cathexis and the self. *J Consult Psychol, 17*:343-347, 1953.
29. STROEM, R.: Physical fitness, self-esteem and attitudes toward physical activity. Paper presented at the American Association of Health, Physical Education and Recreation, National Convention, Boston, Mass., April, 1969.
30. SWENSON, C. H.: Empirical evaluation of human figure drawings, 1957, *Psychol Bull, 70*:20-44, 1968.

31. WEATHERFORD, R. S., AND HORROCKS, J.: Peer acceptance and over and under achievement in school. *J Psychol, 66*:215-220, 1967.
32. ZELLER, JANET: Relationships between parental attitudes about physical education and their children's performance in physical tasks. M.A. Thesis, University of California, Los Angeles, 1968.
33. ZELLER, JANET: Comparison of normals to children with diagnosed indices of minimal neurological dysfunction, using the Cratty Battery of Perceptual-Motor Tests. Unpublished study, Perceptual-Motor Learning Laboratory, University of California, Los Angeles, 1967.

Chapter II

GAME CHOICES OF CHILDREN WITH MOVEMENT PROBLEMS

INTRODUCTION

To an increased degree the study of children at play has come to occupy the time of the behavioral scientist (2, 5). Observation of children in game situations has begun to provide important cues concerning their later intellectual and emotional behaviors. At times game behavior has been used to assess personality, and at other times the type selected by various cultures has allowed insights to be made into the nature of the culture in which the games take place (1).

Game participation by children has been said to have several functions, including the "joyful release of energy" and the preparation for adult activities within the culture (2). For example, the children within the culture of the Australian Aborigine are seen to play games requiring manual dexterity similar to the survival skills observed in their parents. In addition to specific types of skills of this nature, the general nature of the games played suggests the nature of the adult society into which the child will be projected. Highly competitive cultures elicit games of skill, strategy and strength from their young, while cultures heavily permeated by religious and mystical symbolism seem to encourage games of chance from their children. The young in various subcultures within larger, more complex societies can often be counted upon to play games which reflect the strata in which they find themselves. For example, it has been suggested that children and adults within lower socioeconomic classes in the United States engage more in games of chance than in games of strategy and skill, as it is sometimes felt among members of this group that they stand little chance of success in competitive matters, while "lady luck" will smile equally on the poor and rich alike.

Several trends are beginning to emerge in the study of game choices of children in the American culture. For example, it has recently been speculated that to an increasing degree young children in the United States are beginning to devise games more heavily laden with intellectual components than with vigorous muscular effort. The children of this culture seem to be perceiving and preparing for the exercise of their cognitive facilities which they believe will lead to success as adults rather than endurance, strength and/or manual skill.*

A second trend is beginning to emerge to an increased degree: girls within the American culture play later in childhood than they formerly did, the vigorous games similar to those played by the boys.

Games provide important insights into childhood behavior. For example, by noting how some children play games, and the type of games they play, other children tend to form personality assessments of their peers. The choices of games a child selects to participate in have been employed by several investigators as measures of gender identification. Tests by Brown, Lefkowitz, Sutton-Smith and others are examples of these (6).

For the past few years a modification of the Sutton-Smith Games Choice Test has been administered to children participating in a program of movement education at the University of California at Los Angeles. This short-form of the test was developed in order to exclude games on the original which were not usually played by children in Southern California. At the same time, the measure was obtained to survey possible gender identification problems in children, and to determine the scope and nature of the games played by the children served by the program.

This study had as its primary purpose a survey of the responses to the questionnaire elicited from an elementary school

---

* Dr. Brian Sutton-Smith of the Teacher's College, Columbia University, New York. A speech presented to the North American Society of Sport Psychology in Washington D. C., October, 1968.

population, matched according to age and sex to a group of children with motor problems. Other comparisons of age trends are also surveyed in this investigation.

It was hypothesized that boys with movement problems would tend in childhood to avoid vigorous games and games requiring manual dexterities. It was further assumed that significant sex differences would be obtained between the percent of boys and girls from the so-called normal population reporting participation in the various games and activities contained on the inquiry form employed in this investigation. It was further believed that the responses of the boys with movement problems concerning game participation would to a large degree tend to parallel the responses received from the population of normal girls.

PROCEDURES

The revised questionnaire was administered over a two-year period to 199 boys and 34 girls evaluated on a number of other motor and perceptual tests for admission to a program at UCLA for the remediation of coordination difficulties. The majority of these children had evidenced positive neurological "soft-signs" when evaluated in a neurological examination. They were, as a group, significantly below normal populations in measures of balance agility, ball handling ability, drawing accuracy and the like. In addition, these children and their parents reported that the children encountered difficulties when attempting to interact socially in the usual childhood games.

In the spring of 1969 the same questionnaire was administered to 293 children at an elementary school adjacent to the University. The children at this school were from a socioeconomic group similar to that from which the children with moderate coordination problems were gleaned. They were served in the program previously outlined. The administration of the test to this second group of normal children, however, was not carried out individually, but in a group situation.

The age and sex breakdown of this population is as follows adjacent ages were grouped together to afford larger numbers when making later statistical comparisons):

	Ages			
	5-6	7-8	9-10	11-12
Boys	18	58	44	12	Total 132
Girls	36	73	45	7	Total 161

A survey of the questionnaire results following these two administrations was carried out, and the percent of responses answered by the total control (normal) group by sex and age was computed. Additionally, the scores from a subgroup totaling one hundred thirty-eight children from this initial population, matched by age and sex, were compared to the responses elicited from a similar number of children with moderate motor problems who had also been surveyed. The age and sex breakdown of these matched groups were as follows:

	Ages							
	5	6	7	8	9	10	11	12
Boys	1	17	20	25	20	10	9	3	Total 105
Girls	3	2	1	10	6	5	5	1	Total 33

The mean ages of the children in the matched groups were as follows: boys' mean age 8.20 years (S.D.=1.63), girls' mean age 8.63 years (S.D.=1.82).

The mean age of the boys in the normal population of one hundred thirty-two boys was 8.32 years (S.D.=1.74), and the mean age of the one hundred sixty-one girls in the same population was 7.78 (S.D.=1.56).

Classification of Games

Games and play activities of children have been subjected to several classification systems. For example, Caillois has suggested that four categories of games exist, including games in which competition is paramount (Agon), games of chance (Alea), games of pretense (Mimicry) and games in which the child attempts to seek satisfying vertigo (Ilinx) (1).

For the purposes of this investigation the games of the questionnaire utilized were placed into one of eight classifications:

1. *Games exclusive to childhood* (C): wall dodgeball,

marbles, hopscotch, jump rope, London Bridge, seesaw, jacks, drop the handkerchief, farmer in the dell, ring around the rosy and mother may I?

2. *Games in which the child is preparing for or imitating parallel and existent adult functions* (*A*): house, doctors, cowboys, hunting, cars, spaceman, toy trains, dance, dolls, making model airplanes, store and mother may I?

3. *Games requiring manipulative behavior, fine coordination* (*F*): marbles, cooking, jacks, making model airplanes, sewing and using tools.

4. *Games involving activity of the larger muscles* (*B*): wall dodgeball, hopscotch, jump rope, boxing, bowling, London Bridge, building forts, wrestling, football, seesaw, drop the handkerchief, ring around the rosy and musical chairs.

5. *Activities requiring aiming and steadiness* (*S*): shooting, bows and arrows, darts and bowling.

6. *Activities paralleling adult recreational interests* (*R*): hunting, bowling, bows and arrows and shooting.

7. *Musical games* (*M*): London Bridge, dance, farmer in the dell, ring around the rosy and musical chairs.

8. *Games involving some kind of obvious or subtle agression* (*A*): hunting, cowboys, soldiers, cops and robbers, bandits, build forts, boxing, shooting, bows and arrows, football and wrestling.

Additionally, the originators of the test assigned either a "masculine" or "feminine" score to each of the items it contained. A comparison of the games in the categories above to the classification of the games by sex was carried out to afford additional insight into the nature of childhood games participated in by boys and girls in our culture.

FINDINGS

Comparison of the sex categories assigned to each game by the originator of the questionnaire with the eight categories specified above revealed the following:

TABLE VII

Classification of Games	Masculine	Feminine
1. Games exclusive to childhood	wall dodgeball, marbles	hopscotch, seesaw, jump rope, jacks, London Bridge, drop the handkerchief, ring around the rosy, mother may I? farmer in the dell
2. Games imitating adult life functions	cowboys, spaceman, hunting, model airplanes, toy trains, cars	doctors, dolls, house, store, dance, cooking, mother may I?
3. Manipulative behavior	marbles, using tools, model airplanes	cooking, jacks, sewing
4. Large muscle activity	wall dodgeball, boxing, bowling, football, building forts	hopscotch, jump rope, London Bridge, seesaw, musical chairs, ring around the rosy, drop the handkerchief
5. Aiming and steadiness	shooting, darts, bows and arrows, bowling	
6. Parallel adult recreation	hunting, bowling, bows and arrows, shooting	
7. Musical games		dance, farmer in the dell, ring around the rosy, London Bridge, musical chairs
8. Games of aggression	hunting, cowboys, soldiers, cops and robbers, bandits, boxing, build forts, shooting, bows and arrows, wrestling, football	

If one may make the somewhat tenuous assumption that the games on the questionnaire are a representative cross-section of those played by children in the American culture, and that the feminine or masculine connotation assigned to each by the originators of the questionnaire are valid, various hypotheses can be formulated. It is interesting to note, for example, the absence of games of aggression under the feminine category. Apparently the American male may and does play games involving various kinds of aggressive overtones, while the female is not as inclined to do so. Upon surveying Table VII, the girls seem, instead, more involved in games in which music plays a part.

It is also of some interest to note that games preparing children for adult functions are almost equally divided, but that the girls tend to play the role of "doctor" or "storekeeper" more as children than do the boys, whereas later in life most individuals actually assuming these two roles in our society are males.

Again there is a complete division between the sexes when activities requiring aiming and steadiness are listed and compared to the sex classification given to them by Sutton-Smith.* Apparently the ability to maintain a steady hand is more prized among boys, or, perhaps, among men in our culture than among girls and women, or maybe this kind of bias shows up in our chart by some chance. In any case, further research on this topic might be enlightening.

Inspection of categories three and four reveals that both boys and girls play games involving both fine and gross motor skill. It is sometimes assumed that the boys cleave more toward the involvement of the larger muscles, whereas girls prefer games requiring manipulative abilities; however, it is also true that most games require both fine and gross motor skill in almost equal combinations, i.e., "basketball" requires a fine touch when dribbling the ball, plus jumping and running abilities when moving down the floor; "bowling" similarly requires control of both the large and small muscles. Thus, attempting to separate either childhood or adult games into neat categories employing the use of either the larger or smaller muscles is, at best, not a very exact undertaking.

This questionnaire seems to contain more games which are feminine in nature which are exclusive to childhood, whereas only "wall dodgeball" and "marbles" among the masculine games were designated as exclusive to childhood. It might be assumed that more of the games played by boys in childhood in our culture represent preparation for the wide variety of adult roles into which boys might project themselves, as opposed to the relatively fewer roles open to many women, as reflected in game choice, i.e., "sewing" and "cooking." It would be interest-

---

* These classifications, of course, were not made in an arbitrary manner as were the eight categories arrived at by the present authors; whether a game was classified as "feminine" or "masculine" depended upon whether or not it was found to be usually participated in by one or the other sex to a greater degree.

ing to compare game choices in this category among girls from various socioeconomic groups.

It also appears that boys are more likely to play games which in some way prepare them for adult recreational activities, whereas girls games seem to be terminal to a larger degree. Again, further, more penetrating research might explore this hypothesis more fully.

Age and Sex Differences in the Normal Population of Children (N = 264)

Boys' Choices

Table VIII reveals the percent of positive responses ("I like to play the game") to the various items on the questionnaire on the part of the 132 boys by age in the normal population. As can be seen when surveying the game choices of the total male population, the most frequently mentioned games and activities are "using tools" (94%), "bowling" (90%), "playing football" (87%), "shooting" (29%), and "making model airplanes" (89%).

Marked shifts in voiced preferences may also be seen as a function of age, upon consulting this table. There is a general trend following the age of six years, as would be expected, for the boys' shift away from the so-called "feminine" games. Forty-four percent of the boys between the ages of five and six years reported playing "store," while only approximately 17 percent of the boys between the ages of eleven and twelve years reported doing so. "Mother may I?" was reported by 61 percent of the younger boys of five and six years, whereas only 8 percent of the older boys of eleven and twelve years reported doing so. Seventy-seven percent of the younger boys said that they played "musical chairs," while only 17 percent of the older boys reported participating in this game.

Other age trends on Table VIII indicate a shift away from games participated in early childhood independent of any gender component. For example, 44 percent of the boys participated in "cowboys" at the ages of five and six, while only 8 percent reported playing this game from eleven to twelve years of age. Seventy-seven percent of the boys in early childhood reported

TABLE VIII

PERCENT OF BOYS BY AGE WITHIN NORMAL POPULATION (N = 132)
REPORTING PARTICIPATION IN THE GAMES
AND ACTIVITIES POLLED

Games	Age	5-6 (N=18) %	7-8 (N=58) %	9-10 (N=44) %	11-12 (N=12) %	Total (N=132) %
1. Soldiers		44	47	39	25	42
2. House		22	3	2	0	5
3. Doctors		39	29	14	17	24
4. Cowboys		61	41	14	8	32
5. Hunting		94	71	61	67	70
6. Cars		67	53	30	33	45
7. Cops and robbers		83	38	25	17	38
8. Wall dodgeball		56	69	84	58	71
9. Marbles		78	52	41	42	51
10. Hopscotch		33	17	43	50	31
11. Use tools		100	93	91	100	94
12. Jump rope		28	10	23	17	17
13. Boxing		89	72	57	67	69
14. Bowling		78	93	95	83	91
15. Bandits		33	36	6	8	23
16. Spaceman		67	53	16	25	40
17. London Bridge		28	10	2	0	9
18. Cooking		50	16	39	58	32
19. Build forts		72	90	61	58	75
20. Toy trains		78	50	45	33	51
21. Darts		78	90	95	92	90
22. Dance		11	14	18	17	15
23. Wrestling		72	83	77	58	78
24. Sewing		22	10	20	8	15
25. Seesaw		44	40	9	17	28
26. Football		83	84	93	83	87
27. Dolls		11	0	4	0	3
28. Bows and arrows		94	83	82	83	84
29. Shooting		78	81	82	83	81
30. Jacks		28	22	18	8	20
31. Make model airplanes		83	95	84	92	89
32. Drop the handkerchief		44	12	2	33	14
33. Store		44	16	11	17	18
34. Farmer in the dell		33	10	2	0	10
35. Ring around the rosy		33	10	2	25	12
36. Mother may I?		61	34	14	8	29
37. Musical chairs		78	51	43	17	51

playing "marbles" while only 42 percent of the older boys reported doing so.

It should be emphasized, however, that this sample is in no way representative of what would be considered a normal

TABLE IX

PERCENT OF GIRLS BY AGE WITHIN NORMAL POPULATION (N = 161)
REPORTING PARTICIPATION IN THE GAMES
AND ACTIVITIES POLLED

Games	Age	5-6 (N=36) %	7-8 (N=73) %	9-10 (N=45) %	11-12 (N=7) %	Total (N=161) %
1. Soldiers		17	11	2	14	9
2. House		86	70	29	4	60
3. Doctors		53	40	20	0	35
4. Cowboys		28	12	4	0	13
5. Hunting		67	44	33	57	47
6. Cars		48	16	16	14	23
7. Cops and robbers		36	33	11	14	27
8. Wall dodgeball		17	62	69	86	55
9. Marbles		72	64	31	29	55
10. Hopscotch		89	88	67	71	81
11. Use tools		61	48	69	43	57
12. Jump rope		89	85	78	100	84
13. Boxing		11	14	8	14	12
14. Bowling		61	63	76	100	68
15. Bandits		25	15	6	0	14
16. Spaceman		22	11	4	0	11
17. London Bridge		86	48	16	14	46
18. Cooking		92	90	91	86	91
19. Build forts		33	55	38	43	45
20. Toy trains		42	22	8	14	22
21. Darts		56	68	67	71	65
22. Dance		83	79	80	86	81
23. Wrestling		31	30	44	29	34
24. Sewing		83	84	80	86	83
25. Seesaw		89	64	36	43	61
26. Football		25	30	49	43	35
27. Dolls		75	60	42	43	56
28. Bows and arrows		42	38	38	57	40
29. Shooting		36	30	36	57	34
30. Jacks		72	64	51	57	62
31. Make model airplanes		28	22	24	43	25
32. Drop the handkerchief		70	44	18	0	40
33. Store		81	66	33	14	58
34. Farmer in the dell		70	34	2	14	32
35. Ring around the rosy		86	37	8	14	39
36. Mother may I?		92	70	36	29	63
37. Musical chairs		89	74	47	43	69

population of boys in the United States. They were drawn from a school with a median parent's income of an estimated $20,000 per year.

Girls' Choices

Table IX indicates the percent of the 161 girls reporting participation in the various games. Inspection of Table IX reveals several interesting age trends in the data. For example, there was increased participation in "bowling" from only 61 percent reporting participation in the earlier age bracket, to 100 percent participation in the oldest division surveyed. This final percent is undoubtedly a reflection of the socioeconomic group polled, as well as the increased ability of the girls to handle the weight of the ball.

The more childish games diminish in popularity as the responses of the older girls are compared to those collected from the youngest. Eighty-eight percent of the girls at five to six years of age said that they played seesaw, while by eleven and twelve years, only 43 percent reported doing so. Similar trends are noted when inspecting the percentages of younger and older girls participating in "jacks," "doctor" and "ring around the rosy."

Other feminine games apparently remained reasonably popular all through childhood. Over 80 percent of the girls reported "dancing" at all ages; "cooking" and "hopscotch" also remained popular with girls at all ages, with over 80 percent of all age groups reporting participation in these latter two activities.

TABLE X

COMPARISON OF RESPONSES, BY SEX, OF THE CHILDREN (N = 138)
WITHIN THE NORMAL POPULATION WHO REPORTED
PARTICIPATING IN THE VARIOUS GAMES
AND ACTIVITIES

Games	Boys (N = 105) %	Girls (N = 33) %	t
1. Soldiers	38	9	4.26*
2. House	5	45	4.49*
3. Doctors	25	21	.47
4. Cowboys	29	6	3.83*
5. Hunting	70	39	3.26*
6. Cars	45	27	1.98
7. Cops and robbers	31	21	2.00
8. Wall dodgeball	73	75	.23
9. Marbles	49	54	.61
10. Hopscotch	29	75	5.29*
11. Use tools	90	66	2.76*
12. Jump rope	16	75	7.11*

13.	Boxing	71	21	5.75*
14.	Bowling	91	69	2.59
15.	Bandits	23	12	1.60
16.	Spaceman	40	3	6.61*
17.	London Bridge	9	33	2.80*
18.	Cooking	31	90	8.55*
19.	Build forts	75	42	3.48*
20.	Toy trains	49	18	3.78*
21.	Darts	88	69	2.21
22.	Dance	15	81	8.68*
23.	Wrestling	77	42	3.68*
24.	Sewing	14	84	9.72*
25.	Seesaw	27	48	2.16
26.	Football	88	39	5.44*
27.	Dolls	2	60	6.10*
28.	Bows and arrows	83	36	5.16*
29.	Shooting	82	30	5.91*
30.	Jacks	17	63	5.05*
31.	Make model airplanes	90	36	6.14*
32.	Drop the handkerchief	14	36	2.44
33.	Store	17	42	2.69*
34.	Farmer in the dell	11	27	1.93
35.	Ring around the rosy	10	24	1.78
36.	Mother may I?	30	51	2.16
37.	Musical chairs	48	63	1.54

* Differences significant at 5 percent level.

Boy-Girl Comparisons Within the Normal Population

Table X contains a comparison of the percent of boys and girls within the total population who reported participation in various games and activities contained on the survey form.

A survey of Table X indicates that, as expected, the reports of the girls and those of the boys evidenced significant differences in certain of the games and activities shown on the game choice form. A significantly greater percent of the boys than the girls reported playing and participating in "spaceman," "building forts," "wrestling," "football," "bows and arrows," "shooting" and "making model airplanes." On the other hand, significantly more of the girls reported playing and participating in "store," "jacks," "dolls," "sewing," "cooking," "London Bridge," "jump rope," "hopscotch" and "house."

Relatively equal participation was reported by both the girls and boys within the population surveyed in "cars," "cops and robbers," "wall dodgeball," "marbles," "darts," "musical chairs" and "mother may I?". This kind of finding, if found to be consistent in larger and more representative populations of children, would suggest that a more penetrating look might be taken at the manner in which boy-girl reports obtained in these latter activities truly reflect some kind of gender identification problem, and/or the extent to which these activities may be classified as "masculine" or "feminine."

Responses of Children With Movement Problems to the Game Choice Test

The results of responses from 105 boys with moderate motor problems (age range 5 to 12, mean age 8.2 years; S.D. 1.63) were obtained, as were the responses of thirty-three girls (range 5 to 12 years, mean age 8.63 years; S.D. 1.82) with similar problems to the games choice test. Again the expected sex differences are seen to emerge in the obviously "masculine" and "feminine" activities as depicted in Table XI.

TABLE XI

PERCENT OF THE BOYS AND GIRLS (N = 138) WITH MODERATE MOTOR PROBLEMS REPORTING PARTICIPATION IN THE VARIOUS GAMES AND ACTIVITIES POLLED

Games	*Boys (N = 105)* %	*Girls (N = 33)* %	*t*
1. Soldiers	44	15	3.72*
2. House	30	66	3.87*
3. Doctors	48	54	.61
4. Cowboys	46	18	3.41*
5. Hunting	52	36	1.67
6. Cars	68	27	4.61*
7. Cops and robbers	49	27	2.42*
8. Wall dodgeball	72	87	2.05
9. Marbles	55	60	.51
10. Hopscotch	42	72	3.30*
11. Use tools	84	54	3.24*
12. Jump rope	33	87	7.28*
13. Boxing	48	18	3.66*
14. Bowling	81	42	4.15*
15. Bandits	34	12	3.01*
16. Spaceman	48	12	4.86*
17. London Bridge	34	60	2.68*
18. Cooking	51	75	2.70*
19. Build forts	74	54	2.08

20.	Toy trains	71	51	2.06*
21.	Darts	83	51	3.40*
22.	Dance	25	75	5.81*
23.	Wrestling	56	27	3.19*
24.	Sewing	26	69	4.72*
25.	Seesaw	50	66	1.68
26.	Football	63	36	2.84*
27.	Dolls	10	63	6.02*
28.	Bows and arrows	73	45	2.92*
29.	Shooting	70	33	3.98*
30.	Jacks	40	63	2.40*
31.	Make model airplanes	78	6	12.63*
32.	Drop the handkerchief	23	36	1.40
33.	Store	52	72	2.17
34.	Farmer in the dell	23	54	2.21
35.	Ring around the rosy	32	51	1.94
36.	Mother may I?	29	87	7.95*
37.	Musical chairs	60	78	2.09

* Differences significant at 5 percent level.

TABLE XII

PERCENT OF THE GIRLS, BY AGE, WITHIN THE POPULATION OF
CHILDREN WITH MODERATE MOTOR PROBLEMS REPORTING
PARTICIPATION IN THE VARIOUS GAMES AND
ACTIVITIES POLLED (N = 34)

Games	Age	5-6 (N = 5) %	7-8 (N = 11) %	9-10 (N = 11) %	11-12 (N = 7) %	Total (N = 34) %
1. Soldiers		20	18	9	14	15
2. House		80	82	55	57	68
3. Doctors		60	64	55	29	53
4. Cowboys		40	27	9	0	18
5. Hunting		60	55	27	0	35
6. Cars		60	27	18	14	26
7. Cops and robbers		80	27	18	0	26
8. Wall dodgeball		60	91	100	86	88
9. Marbles		100	64	45	57	62
10. Hopscotch		80	82	73	57	74
11. Use tools		40	55	64	43	53
12. Jump rope		100	91	82	86	88
13. Boxing		20	18	18	14	18
14. Bowling		60	36	55	29	44
15. Bandits		20	18	0	14	12
16. Spaceman		20	18	9	0	12
17. London Bridge		100	73	36	57	62
18. Cooking		60	82	73	86	76
19. Build forts		80	36	45	71	53
20. Toy trains		80	55	36	43	50
21. Darts		40	64	55	43	53

22.	Dance	100	82	64	71	76
23.	Wrestling	40	27	18	29	26
24.	Sewing	60	91	73	43	71
25.	Seesaw	80	73	55	71	68
26.	Football	40	36	27	43	35
27.	Dolls	80	73	55	57	65
28.	Bows and arrows	40	27	55	57	44
29.	Shooting	60	36	27	14	32
30.	Jacks	40	82	64	57	65
31.	Make model airplanes	0	18	0	0	5
32.	Drop the handkerchief	20	73	9	29	35
33.	Store	100	91	55	57	74
34.	Farmer in the dell	100	64	36	43	56
35.	Ring around the rosy	100	73	27	29	53
36.	Mother may I?	80	91	100	71	88
37.	Musical chairs	100	82	64	86	79

Age trends within the female and male populations of children with moderate motor problems are shown in Tables XI and XII.

A consideration of the data contained in Table XII indicates that the girls with moderate motor problems tend to remain high and consistent in their reports of playing "house," "wall dodgeball," "dance," "seesaw" and the various feminine musical games typical of childhood.

The data collected from the boys with moderate motor problems, Table XIII, indicate consistent and high participation in "bowling"; however, in general, the boys tended to drop off in their reported participation in such activities as "seesaw," "spaceman," "hopscotch," "cowboys," "doctors" and "soldiers" as they grew older.

TABLE XIII

PERCENT OF THE BOYS, BY AGE, WITHIN THE POPULATION OF CHILDREN WITH MODERATE MOTOR PROBLEMS REPORTING PARTICIPATION IN THE VARIOUS GAMES AND ACTIVITIES POLLED (N = 199)

Games	Age	5-6 (N = 32) %	7-8 (N = 73) %	9-10 (N = 56) %	11-12 (N = 38) %	Total (N = 199) %
1. Soldiers		53	48	59	24	47
2. House		69	30	32	3	32
3. Doctors		75	53	63	18	53
4. Cowboys		66	44	41	13	41
5. Hunting		59	60	48	18	49

6.	Cars	72	74	71	47	68
7.	Cops and robbers	44	49	55	26	46
8.	Wall dodgeball	53	71	82	53	68
9.	Marbles	69	56	55	24	52
10.	Hopscotch	59	41	41	24	41
11.	Use tools	78	85	80	71	80
12.	Jump rope	38	33	34	29	33
13.	Boxing	47	49	63	29	49
14.	Bowling	63	73	83	82	75
15.	Bandits	53	32	43	13	35
16.	Spaceman	63	53	54	32	51
17.	London Bridge	67	41	25	3	33
18.	Cooking	50	37	48	29	41
19.	Build forts	72	73	73	42	67
20.	Toy trains	81	71	71	34	66
21.	Darts	56	81	90	74	78
22.	Dance	44	25	43	26	33
23.	Wrestling	53	58	66	58	60
24.	Sewing	50	21	25	3	23
25.	Seesaw	69	56	46	18	48
26.	Football	41	73	77	65	68
27.	Dolls	28	8	7	3	10
28.	Bows and arrows	66	75	75	47	68
29.	Shooting	75	74	79	53	71
30.	Jacks	44	40	38	13	35
31.	Make model airplanes	72	79	79	82	78
32.	Drop the handkerchief	44	34	23	7	28
33.	Store	72	59	61	18	54
34.	Farmer in the dell	63	36	20	8	30
35.	Ring around the rosy	59	34	29	8	32
36.	Mother may I?	63	40	32	16	37
37.	Musical chairs	63	60	63	29	55

Matched Group Comparisons

Children With Motor Problems Versus Children From a Normal Population

Of importance in this investigation was a determination of whether significant differences existed in the percent of children with moderate problems reporting participation in the various games, and the participation reported by children from within a so-called normal population of youngsters. Table XIV contains the data which illustrate this comparison and is composed of responses from 105 boys from each group matched by age.

TABLE XIV

COMPARISONS OF PERCENT OF BOYS WITH MOTOR PROBLEMS
REPORTING GAME PARTICIPATION TO THE PERCENT OF
BOYS FROM NORMAL POPULATION REPORTING
GAME PARTICIPATION

		Normal %	*Motor Problems* %	*Difference* %	*t*
1.	Soldiers	38	44	6	.90
2.	House	5	30	25	5.10*
3.	Doctors	25	48	23	3.59*
4.	Cowboys	29	46	17	2.61
5.	Hunting	70	52	18	2.72*
6.	Cars	45	68	23	3.48*
7.	Cops and robbers	38	49	11	1.64
8.	Wall dodgeball	73	72	1	.16
9.	Marbles	49	55	6	.88
10.	Hopscotch	29	42	13	2.00
11.	Use tools	90	84	6	1.30
12.	Jump rope	16	33	17	2.93*
13.	Boxing	71	48	23	3.53*
14.	Bowling	91	81	10	2.12
15.	Bandits	23	34	9	1.47
16.	Spaceman	40	48	8	1.19
17.	London Bridge	9	34	25	4.62*
18.	Cooking	31	51	20	3.03*
19.	Build forts	75	74	1	.17
20.	Toy trains	49	71	22	3.38*
21.	Darts	88	83	5	1.04
22.	Dance	15	25	10	1.81
23.	Wrestling	77	56	21	3.33*
24.	Sewing	14	26	12	2.22
25.	Seesaw	27	50	23	3.53*
26.	Football	88	63	25	4.46*
27.	Dolls	2	10	8	2.50
28.	Bows and arrows	83	73	10	1.78
29.	Shooting	82	70	12	2.06
30.	Jacks	17	40	23	3.83*
31.	Make model airplanes	90	78	12	2.44
32.	Drop the handkerchief	14	23	9	1.69
33.	Store	17	52	35	5.83*
34.	Farmer in the dell	11	23	12	2.40
35.	Ring around the rosy	10	32	22	4.07*
36.	Mother may I?	30	29	1	.16
37.	Musical chairs	48	60	12	1.76

* Differences significant at 5 percent level.

Inspection of Table XIV indicates that significant differences in the reports extended by the boys with problems in movement and by the boys within the purportedly normal population were obtained in fifteen out of the thirty-seven activities contained on the game-choice questionnaire. On the one hand, the boys with motor problems reported significantly greater participation in such activities as "doctors," "house," "cars," "London Bridge," "jump rope," "toy trains," "seesaw," "jacks," "store," "cooking" and "ring-around the rosy." As will be noted, nine out of ten of these activities (the exception being "toy trains") are designated as feminine by the originators of the games choice test; while at the same time, as can be seen in Table X, significantly more of the girls and the boys within the normal population in this investigation reported playing six of these eight activities ("doctors," "house," "jump rope," "cooking," "jacks," and "playing store").

The boys with motor problems, as a group, seemed to avoid participation in the more vigorous games on the list when their responses were compared to those obtained from the matched group from a so-called "normal" population (Table XIV). Significantly fewer of the former reported playing "football," "wrestling" and "boxing." It is a common observation that individuals avoid doing what they cannot do well. It thus was found, as expected, that the boys with motor problems tended as a group to restrict their choices to the more passive and feminine activities while at the same time they avoided the more vigorous ones, all of which involve some degree of body contact.

At the same time it should be noted that no significant differences in percent of participation between the two groups was noted when their responses about playing "wall dodgeball" were tabulated. The differences in responses to questions about two out of the three manipulative activities, i.e., "making model airplanes" and "using tools," which appear on the questionnaire, while not significant are in the expected direction.

These findings may be subjected to an interesting analysis. One may compare the activities designated as usually participated in by girls (by the originators of the questionnaire) to the activities selected by the group of boys with motor problems. Another comparison can be made between the questionnaire responses of the boys with motor problems and the girls within the so-called "normal" population of youngsters surveyed.

For example, the originators of the questionnaire designate the following activities as feminine:

House	Sewing	Store
Doctors	Seesaw	Farmer in the dell
Hopscotch	Dolls	Ring around the rosy
Jump rope	Jacks	Mother may I?
London Bridge	Drop the handkerchief	Musical chairs
Cooking	Dance	

When the responses of the normal girls were compared to those of the normal boys the following activities were more often named by the girls (see Table X):

House	Seesaw
Wall dodgeball	Dolls
Marbles	Jacks
Hopscotch	Drop the handkerchief
Jump rope	Store
London bridge	Farmer in the dell
Cooking	Ring around the rosy
Dance	Mother may I?
Sewing	Musical chairs

Third, when the responses of the boys with motor problems were compared to those within the normal population these activities appeared more likely to be participated in by the boys who evidence coordination problems.

Soldiers	Toy trains
House	Dance
Doctors	Sewing
Cowboys	Seesaw
Cars	Dolls
Marbles	Jacks
Hopscotch	Drop the handkerchief
Jump rope	Store
Bandits	Farmer in the dell
Spaceman	Ring around the rosy
London Bridge	Musical chairs
Cooking	

The similarity of the three lists is apparent. The final list contains "dolls," "sewing," "ring around the rosy," "farmer in the dell" and similar feminine activities. The only masculine activities contained on it include those in which there seems to be some kind of projection into a hero and/or aggressive role ("spaceman," "soldiers," "cowboys," and "bandits"). The boys with motor problems, on the other hand, seem to carefully avoid direct tests of their vigor and motor capacities in the three contact activities placed on the list ("boxing," "wrestling" and "football").

Comparisons of Matched Groups of Girls

Table XV contains the results of a comparison between thirty-three girls who evidenced motor problems versus thirty-three girls, similar in age, in a population of so-called "normal" children. The mean age of the two groups was 8.63 (S.D. 1.83). The range was from five to twelve years.

TABLE XV

COMPARISON OF PERCENT OF GIRLS WITH MOTOR PROBLEMS
REPORTING GAME PARTICIPATION TO THE PERCENT OF
GIRLS FROM NORMAL POPULATION REPORTING
GAME PARTICIPATION

		Normal %	Motor Problem %	Difference %	t
1.	Soldiers	9	15	6	.75
2.	House	45	66	21	1.76
3.	Doctors	21	54	33	2.89*
4.	Cowboys	6	18	12	1.53
5.	Hunting	39	36	3	.25
6.	Cars	27	27	0	0
7.	Cops and robbers	21	27	6	.57
8.	Wall dodgeball	75	87	12	1.26
9.	Marbles	54	60	14	1.16
10.	Hopscotch	75	72	3	.27
11.	Use tools	66	54	12	1.00
12.	Jump rope	75	87	12	1.26
13.	Boxing	21	18	3	.30
14.	Bowling	69	42	27	2.30
15.	Bandits	12	12	0	0
16.	Spaceman	3	12	9	1.42
17.	London Bridge	33	60	27	2.28
18.	Cooking	90	75	15	1.64
19.	Build forts	42	54	12	.98

20.	Toy trains	18	51	33	3.02*
21.	Darts	69	51	18	1.52
22.	Dance	81	75	6	.59
23.	Wrestling	42	27	15	1.30
24.	Sewing	84	69	15	1.47
25.	Seesaw	48	66	18	1.51
26.	Football	39	36	3	.25
27.	Dolls	60	63	3	.25
28.	Bows and arrows	36	45	9	.75
29.	Shooting	30	33	3	.26
30.	Jacks	63	63	0	0
31.	Make model airplanes	36	6	30	3.22
32.	Drop the handkerchief	36	36	0	0
33.	Store	42	72	30	2.58
34.	Farmer in the dell	27	54	27	2.32
35.	Ring around the rosy	24	51	27	2.36
36.	Mother may I?	51	87	36	3.41*
37.	Musical chairs	63	78	15	1.36

* Differences significant at 5 percent level.

Due to the limited number of subjects, few of the differences in percentages are statistically significant on Table XV. However, the data suggest that the girls with movement problems, as a group, tend to avoid "making models" and "using tools," and to "sew" less, while at the same time they participate more in the five feminine games at the end of the list ("store," "farmer in the dell," "ring around the rosy," "mother may I?" and "musical chairs"). The girls with movement problems do not seem to avoid some of the more vigorous games such as "wall dodgeball" nor do they apparently withdraw from "cooking."

Comparisons of the Percent of Normal Boys, Boys With Movement Problems and Normal Girls Selecting Various Games, as a Function of Age

To further illustrate some of the findings discussed in the previous sections, the percent of children within three of the groups studied, reporting participation in the various activities, were graphed on the following tables (XVI to XXVIII).* The activities graphed in this manner include three which would be

---

* The percent of girls with movement problems were not graphed by age, as within each age grouping the number of subjects would not permit any valid generalizations to be formulated.

TABLE XVI

PERCENT OF PARTICIPATION REPORTED IN "BOXING," BY AGE, OF
THE NORMAL BOYS AND GIRLS, AND OF THE BOYS
WITH MOVEMENT PROBLEMS

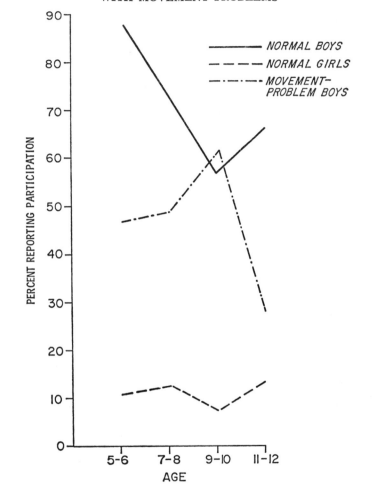

termed vigorous contact sports ("boxing," "football" and "wrestling"), five activities which were assigned (by the data in this
study, as well as by the questionnaire's originators) to the
"feminine" category ("dance," "store," "jacks," "doctor" and
"house"), a manipulative activity ("using tools") and four
activities which might be classified as evidencing some kind
of adventurous imagery on the part of the participants (including

"cars," "cops and robbers," "spaceman" and "bandits"). A fifteenth activity, "hopscotch," was also graphed in this manner to illuminate some interesting trends in the data.

TABLE XVII

PERCENT OF PARTICIPATION REPORTED IN "FOOTBALL," BY AGE, OF THE NORMAL BOYS AND GIRLS, AND OF THE BOYS WITH MOVEMENT PROBLEMS

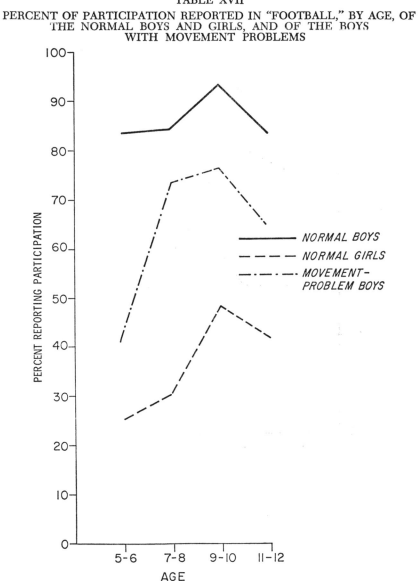

TABLE XVIII

PERCENT OF PARTICIPATION REPORTED IN "WRESTLING," BY AGE,
OF THE NORMAL BOYS AND GIRLS, AND OF THE BOYS
WITH MOVEMENT PROBLEMS

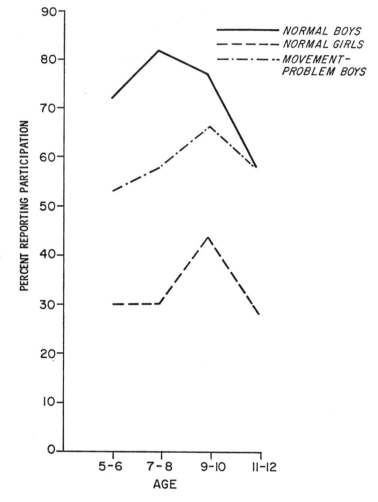

As can be seen by consulting Tables XVI through XIX, the
boys with movement problems tend to avoid these vigorous
activities at each age when compared to the boys from the
so-called "normal" population. In the case of "boxing" (Table
XVI) it appears that the boys with movement problems seemed
to "get themselves up" for an attempt at this type of activity

TABLE XIX

PERCENT OF PARTICIPATION REPORTED IN DOLLS, BY AGE, OF
THE NORMAL BOYS AND GIRLS, AND OF THE BOYS
WITH MOVEMENT PROBLEMS

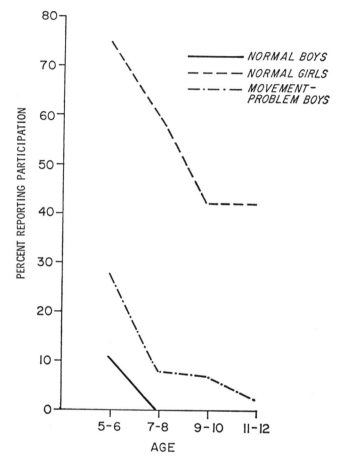

at about the age of nine and a half, but when incurring failure
tend to drop off in their enthusiasm for this activity to a marked
degree by later childhood. At no age did the responses of the
boys with movement problems approach the levels of the boys
from the normal population concerning participation in football
(Table XVII). At the same time, more of the boys with movement problems apparently played this vigorous sport than did
the normal girls. Again in Table XVIII the tendency of boys

TABLE XX

PERCENT OF PARTICIPATION REPORTED IN "DANCING," BY AGE, OF
THE NORMAL BOYS AND GIRLS, AND OF THE BOYS
WITH MOVEMENT PROBLEMS

with movement problems to avoid vigorous contact is noted, particularly in early childhood.

Table XIX indicates the tendency of boys with movement problems to report playing with "dolls" at older ages than would normally be expected on the part of girls. On the whole, however, the percent reporting "doll" play does not approach the percent of positive responses to this question elicited by the normal girls within the various age groups.

Table XX illustrates the increased preference for "dance" on the part of boys with movement problems when compared to the responses of the boys within the normal population. At the same time, the responses of the former do not approach the degree of participation graphed from the normal girls' responses.

TABLE XXI

PERCENT OF PARTICIPATION REPORTED IN "STORE," BY AGE, OF THE NORMAL BOYS AND GIRLS, AND OF THE BOYS WITH MOVEMENT PROBLEMS

TABLE XXII

PERCENT OF PARTICIPATION REPORTED IN "JACKS" BY AGE, OF
THE NORMAL BOYS AND GIRLS, AND OF THE BOYS
WITH MOVEMENT PROBLEMS

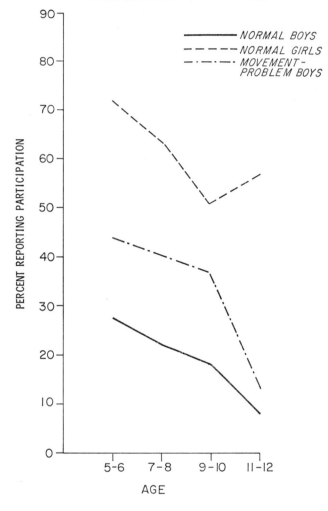

Table XXI, illustrating positive responses to "store" on the part of the three groups, illustrates the close parallel between the girls' responses and those emanating from the boys with movement problems. Table XXII, graphing participation in "jacks," again indicates the tendency for the boys with movement

TABLE XXIII

PERCENT OF PARTICIPATION REPORTED IN "DOCTORS," BY AGE, OF
THE NORMAL BOYS AND GIRLS, AND OF THE BOYS
WITH MOVEMENT PROBLEMS

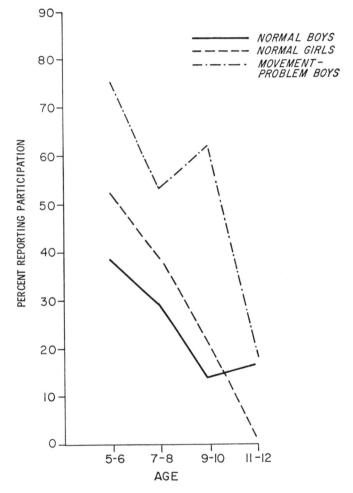

problems to participate in a game enjoyed by a majority of
the girls in childhood. This graph may indicate that upon finding
themselves reasonably unsuccessful in this rather difficult game
involving manual skill, their enthusiasm lagged in later childhood as seen by the drop in participation reported by the eleven

TABLE XXIV

PERCENT OF PARTICIPATION REPORTED IN "PLAYING HOUSE," BY AGE, OF THE NORMAL BOYS AND GIRLS, AND OF THE BOYS WITH MOVEMENT PROBLEMS

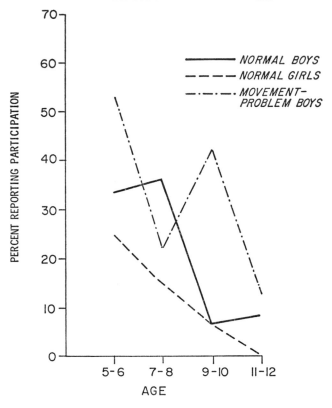

and twelve-year-old inept boys, the majority of whom usually have difficulty in fine motor skills.

Tables XXIII and XXIV again show the tendency of boys with movement problems to "profile" similar to the manner in which normal girls' responses graph. In the case of playing "doctors" it appears that this type of activity is even more popular among boys with coordination problems than with the groups of normal girls surveyed.

Table XXV, graphing the percent of children reporting "using tools," again illustrates the aparent reluctance of many boys with motor problems to engage in activities requiring manual dex-

TABLE XXV

PERCENT OF PARTICIPATION REPORTED IN "USING TOOLS," BY AGE,
OF THE NORMAL BOYS AND GIRLS, AND OF THE BOYS
WITH MOVEMENT PROBLEMS

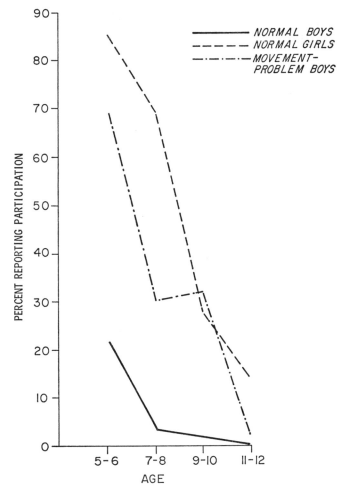

terity. On the other hand, Table XXVI ("cars"), XXVII ("cops and robbers"), XXVIII ("spaceman") and XXIX ("bandits") show, it is believed, the marked tendency of inept boys to project themselves into activities in which they may imagine vigorous movement ("cars") or may act out hero roles ("spaceman," "cops and robbers," etc.). In Table XXVI, "cars," for

TABLE XXVI

PERCENT OF PARTICIPATION REPORTED IN "CARS," BY AGE, OF
THE NORMAL BOYS AND GIRLS, AND OF THE BOYS
WITH MOVEMENT PROBLEMS

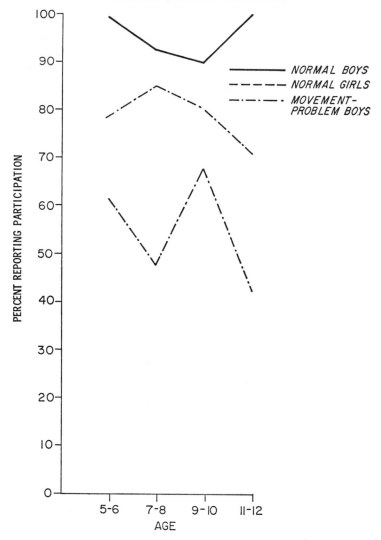

example, the group of uncoordinated boys indicate participation
far in excess of that reported by normal boys and girls. After
early childhood, as Table XXVII indicates, boys with movement
problems report engaging in "cops and robbers" far more often

TABLE XXVII

PERCENT OF PARTICIPATION REPORTED IN "COPS AND ROBBERS,"
BY AGE, OF THE NORMAL BOYS AND GIRLS, AND OF THE BOYS
WITH MOVEMENT PROBLEMS

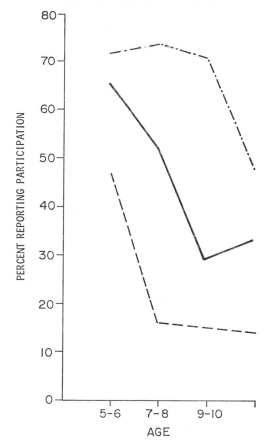

than do normal boys; while Tables XXVII and XXIX ("space-man" and "bandits," respectively) again illustrate the tendency for boys who are not proficient in movement activities to persist in participating in this kind of imagery at older ages than do boys with more obvious and direct ways to manifest their capacities in games.

Table XXX, it is believed, reveals an interesting trend which might be examined further in future research. It would seem that while the boys with movement problems in early childhood

TABLE XXVIII

PERCENT OF PARTICIPATION REPORTED IN "SPACEMAN," BY AGE, OF
THE NORMAL BOYS AND GIRLS, AND OF THE BOYS
WITH MOVEMENT PROBLEMS

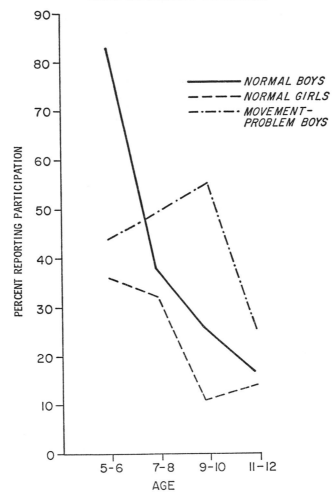

tended more to play "hopscotch" with the girls, by the time
they reached late childhood their motor ineptitude seemed to
reduce their enthusiasm for this reasonably difficult locomotor
activity. This kind of speculation, of course, is rather baseless,
as the data graphed are not reflective of longitudinal trends

TABLE XXIX

PERCENT OF PARTICIPATION REPORTED IN "BANDITS," BY AGE, OF
THE NORMAL BOYS AND GIRLS, AND OF THE BOYS
WITH MOVEMENT PROBLEMS

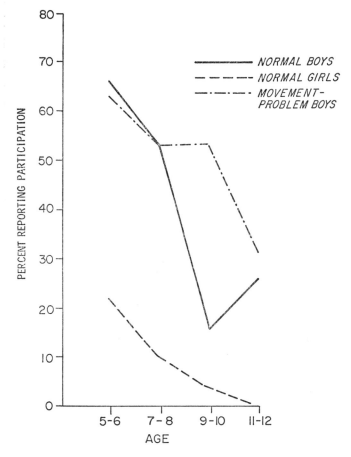

obtained from the responses of the same children over a period
of years, but is cross-sectional data obtained from different
children within the various age groups polled at a single time
in the lives of each.

Summary of the Findings

1. Classification of the games on the questionnaire used,
within eight categories and by the "masculine" and "feminine"
score given them by the originators of the tool, revealed that

TABLE XXX

PERCENT OF PARTICIPATION IN "HOPSCOTCH," BY AGE, OF
THE NORMAL BOYS AND GIRLS, AND OF THE BOYS
WITH MOVEMENT PROBLEMS

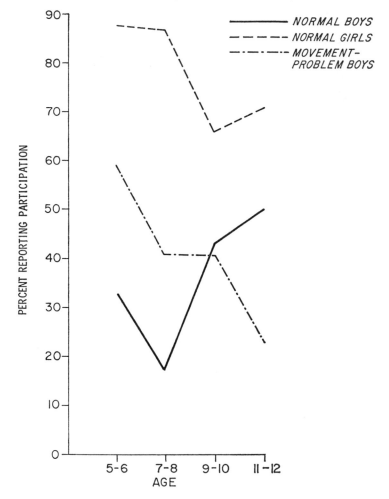

all of the games involving some subtle or direct "aggression"
and those involving "aiming and steadiness" were "masculine"
and all of the musical games were "feminine," while games
requiring large muscle activity were reasonably equally divided
into the "feminine" and "masculine" categories. More games

imitative of later adult functions were played by the boys, with the exception of "doctors" and "store," which were engaged in more by girls yet would probably later become masculine occupations in adulthood. All of the games which were designated as paralleling adult recreational interests were placed into the "masculine" category by the scholars compiling the questionnaire originally.

2. Comparison of girls and boys' responses within the normal population revealed that the most-mentioned games by the males included "using tools," "bowling," "football," "shooting" and "making model airplanes."

3. The percent of responses to game participation classified by age indicated several trends in which, for example, the more passive musical games became less popular among boys as they matured, while the boys tended to adopt more vigorous games as they matured, e.g., "football."

4. The girls' responses within the normal population indicated a preference for "cooking," "hopscotch," and "dancing" at all ages, while some of the more childish musical games tended to diminish in popularity with age.

5. Comparisons of responses by sex within the normal population indicated differences as would be expected by the originators of the questionnaire, with the exception of "cars," "cops and robbers," "wall dodgeball," "marbles," "darts," "musical chairs" and "mother may I?" in which equal participation was indicated.

6. Comparisons of the percent of boys with motor problems versus those from a normal population indicated that the latter group tended to select a pattern of games which was highly similar to that selected by the normal girls.

7. The boys with motor problems tended to avoid selecting vigorous games involving direct contact, such as "football," "wrestling" and "boxing." Rather, the masculine activities they seemed to prefer involved some type of fantasy play in which "pretend" bravery could be evidenced (i.e., "spaceman," "cowboy," "cops and robbers" and the like). It might also be noted that many of these same activities might include a great deal of subtle, indirect aggression.

CONCLUSIONS, IMPLICATIONS AND DISCUSSION
OF THE FINDINGS

In general, it is believed that the data obtained supported the hypotheses initially formulated. It was concluded that, as a group, the boys with motor problems polled in this study avoided participation in vigorous contact activities when compared to boys from a normal population. At the same time these boys tended to seek, to a large degree, the more passive games enjoyed by the normal girls.

The findings, however, revealed several interesting trends which might be explored in further studies. For example, the boys with movement problems seemed to seek an outlet for direct action by participating to a great extent in such games as "spaceman," "cops and robbers" and the like, in which they might imagine themselves brave and vigorous. Likewise, the enjoyment they derived from playing "cars" could also be considered a kind of compensatory behavior for their inability to move well, as in this way they could perhaps move vicariously, through their cars!

Furthermore, it was sometimes seen, as in the case of "hopscotch," that the boys with movement problems during early childhood would seem to seek this feminine game, but upon finding it difficult (or perhaps realizing that it was inappropriate for one of their sex), would tend to participate less in later childhood.

No marked differences were seen when comparing the responses of participation elicited from the girls with movement problems to those received from the so-called normal girls. This was partly due to the number of subjects in the matched groups, and perhaps also to the tendency for the culture to be less punitive to girls for motor ineptitude, a fact which would perhaps be less likely to dampen their enthusiasm for the various activities. The so-called "normal" population was not typical of children within the middle class of American society. Indeed the parents' incomes, estimated at an average of about $20,000 a year, was far in excess of the average salary enjoyed by a family in the United States. It is believed, however, that the so-called normal group used for comparative purposes in this investigation was closely parallel in nature to the makeup of the groups of children with movement problems. The majority of the children taking part in the program at UCLA are from an upper income group, and are drawn from the relatively affluent West Side of Los Angeles adjacent to the University. It is for this reason that while the findings cannot be generalized to socioeconomic groups who are less privileged, at the same time the comparisons between the children from the normal elementary school and those from the program designed to remediate motor difficulties are reasonably valid ones.

Furthermore, the so-called normal population undoubtedly contained a substantial percentage of children with motor problems. A recent investigation suggested that 18.2 percent of so-called normal populations of children consist of children with minimal neurological problems which are reflected in motor incompetencies. Thus the contrasts between the responses of the "normal" and "motor problem" groups might have been even more marked if the children with motor problems had been winnowed out of the former collection of children (4).

It is believed important to be most emphatic concerning the findings relative to the fact that boys with motor problems seemed to prefer passive and "feminine" games. It *is not* felt, for example, that this is necessarily indicative of future sexual maladjustments which might be manifested in adulthood. At the same time, it is believed that these findings indicate an important way in which boys earn social approval and enjoy the interaction of their male peers, which may be to some extent denied the boy with coordination problems. He is subjected to self-assessments and peer assessments and ridicule of his motor ineptitude, and therefore he withdraws from vigorous boys' games. Following his attempts to participate with boys in games it would seem that he may be beset with the following chain of events, which, if not reversed, could lead to moderate or severe problems of personal adjustment. This results in one of three possibilities: (a) participation in girl's games, (b) lack of participation in any games or (c) participation in fantasy games in which movement and bravery is implied and not acted out in direct ways. These three alternatives, in turn, could have several effects: for example, a lack of participation would invariably lead toward a decrease in fitness and skill development; participation with the girls could lead toward the "catching" of feminine mannerisms, which in turn will usually elicit more punishment from their male peers, while participation in the various "brave fantasy" games could have several outcomes including a kind of unpleasant, overcompensatory type of behavior which might bring further ridicule.

It must be noted, however, that a boy who does not participate in vigorous games *need not* be maladjusted, feminine in nature or suffer an inordinate amount of punishment from his peers. While it is perhaps probable that some of the unpleasant outcomes described could occur, they will not invariably transpire. The extent to which a child with motor problems suffers concomitant social adjustment problems involving peer acceptance and gender identification depends upon a number of subtle and obvious factors within the home and environment, including:

1. The values of the parents concerning the importance of participation in active versus inactive (e.g., reading) activities.
2. The values of his most liked and least liked peers.
3. The other attributes the child possesses and is given an opportunity to exploit, i.e. his intellect, artistic abilities and the like.
4. The flexibility of the child's personality and his ability to select and to participate in activities which are more suited to his capabilities, coupled with an ability to shrug off ridicule and criticism.
5. The economic conditions within the home which might permit, for example, an extensive series of private lessons in such socially approved motor skills as swimming and tennis.

It is thus important not to attach too many insidious implications to the findings presented on the previous pages. It is believed, however, that the data presented begin to offer greater insight into the problems encountered by the youths evidencing "the clumsy child syndrome" as they make their way toward adolescence and adulthood. It is hoped, in future studies, to explore some of the questions raised by the findings outlined on these pages.

BIBLIOGRAPHY

1. CAILLOIS, R.: *Man, Play and Games*. Glencoe, Ill., The Free Press of Glencoe, 1961.
2. LOWENFELD, MARGARET: *Play in Childhood*. New York, Wiley, 1967.
3. MACCOBY, ELEANOR E.: *The Development of Sex Differences*. Stanford Calif., Stanford, 1966.
4. RAPPAPORT, SHELDRON R.: *Public Education for Children with Brain Dysfunction*. Syracuse, N. Y., Syracuse, 1969.
5. RAYNOR, JOEL O., AND SMITH, CHARLES P.: Achievement-related motives and risk-taking in games of skill and chance. *J Personality,* 34:176-198, 1966.
6. ROSENBERG, B. G., AND SUTTON-SMITH, B.: The measurement of masculinity and femininity in children. *Child Develop,* 30:373-380, 1959.
7. ROSENBERG, B. G., AND SUTTON-SMITH, B.: A revised conception of masculine-feminine differences in play activity. *J Genet Psychol,* 96:165-170, 1960.
8. SLEE, R. W.: The feminine image factor in girls' attitudes to school subjects. *Brit J Educ Psychol,* 38:212-214, 1968.
9. SUTTON-SMITH, B., AND ROSENBERG, B. G.: *Play and Game List*. Bowling Green, Ohio, Bowling Green State University, 1959.
10. SUTTON-SMITH, B., AND ROSENBERG, B. G.: Sixty years of historical changes in the game preferences of American children. *J Amer Folkl,* 74:17-46, 1961.
11. SUTTON-SMITH, B.; ROSENBERG, B. G., AND MORGAN, E. F.: Development of sex differences in play choices during pre-adolescence. *Child Develop,* 34:119-126, 1963.

Chapter III

CHANGES IN SELECTED PERCEPTUAL-MOTOR ATTRIBUTES OF CHILDREN WITH MODERATE COORDINATION PROBLEMS

INTRODUCTION

THE ANCIENTS WERE the first to discover that the exercise of physical and intellectual capacities leads to change. During the ensuing years educators, and later experimenters, have corroborated these early observations. In most cases, however, physical educators have generally studied rather direct and obvious indices of motor functioning, including strength and cardiovascular endurance. Only within recent years have they begun to investigate the manner in which measures of balance, agility and other measures of movement accuracy may be changed through the introduction of programs of various kinds.

Often these more contemporary studies have explored hypotheses which have suggested that the practice of various motor, sensory-motor, perceptual-motor or visual-motor exercises will improve particular perceptual and/or academic attributes. The investigations by Brown, Lapray and Ross and by Singer, Rutherford and Kershner exemplify this trend (2, 18, 21, 20, 17). Many of these investigators, however, seem to have neglected to determine whether their programs indeed change the attributes they are training in rather direct ways, i.e. motor competency and visual function—but instead attribute measures of intelligence, perceptual competency and emotional health in the batteries given before and after the program of motor therapy whose efficiency they are exploring.

Despite this at-times-illogical methodology, it is generally found that when measured, the programs espoused by Kephart and others (2, 20) do indeed change the attributes inherent in the training methods. It is often unclear, however, whether indeed the changes measured are in truth occurring at very basic levels, for often the training methodologies parallel exactly the items on the pre- and posttests.*

It is felt that if the worth of any program of motor activities is to be properly assessed, it must be ascertained whether participation in the program changes in general ways the attributes which it purports to change, and thus it seems important to determine whether some kind of generalization occurs between, for example, the practice of various tasks which apparently enhance balance and a measure of balance. And it is further felt that the only valid way in which such a change may be evaluated is if the latter measure does not continually appear as a training method.

Another issue which is inherent in the recent studies in which motor function or perceptual-motor competencies have been studied is in the interpretation of the hyphenated term "perceptual-motor" itself. This word had its genesis in the writings of Fleishman and others (12, 7, 9) who used it merely to denote that often when performing so-called motor tasks, there is some kind of involvement of perceptual attributes. When, for example, attempting to follow a "blip" along a radar screen by moving two cursors, one horizontal and the other vertical, which are controlled by hand-manipulated knobs, it is of course necessary to integrate visual input (perceptual) concerning the changing location of the elusive dot and of the location of the cursors with the movements (motor) of the hands on the controlling knobs.

The first listed author of this text utilized the term in this context in his graduate text dealing with movement behavior and motor learning. It is inferred from this use of the term that most of the time the control of reasonably complex voluntary movements is dependent upon some kind of sensory information, from the visual system or from the motor system itself (kinesthetic input).

---

* The first-listed author of this text once reviewed a "research" proposal in which the total program consisted of daily administrations of the test battery, which also was the one involved in the pre- and posttesting program.

Others have interpreted "perceptual-motor" in a different way. Reading that most of the time accurate movement is dependent upon some kind of sensory or perceptual judgments, they have assumed that a cause and effect relationship exists between perception and movement and that thus all motor activities (or perhaps only certain stylized ones which they advocate) contribute in direct ways to all components of perceptual development. This type of "blurred," unprecise speculation has many times encouraged educators, teachers and others dealing with normal and atypical children to place a great deal of faith in various programs of motor activities with the hope that a wide variety of educational and personality ills might be eliminated in various populations of children.*

Within this latter context, it is seldom attempted to define perception nor to delineate in precise terms just what perceptual attributes may change with the introduction of various motor activities, as indeed the authors of statements of this nature seem unfamiliar with the pertinent research on the topic.

It is becoming clear, however, that participation in movement tasks may elicit change in certain perceptual judgments. For example, Hill found that engaging in various one-handed and one-footed movement tasks elicited better left-right discrimination in children (14). At the same time there is little clear-cut evidence that participation in structured or unstructured programs of motor activity significantly changes a wide variety of *visual* perceptual attributes (judgments formed primarily through vision).

The following investigation, therefore, had two primary purposes: to determine whether significant changes could be elicited in selected *motor competencies* of boys evidencing moderate coordination problems, and to ascertain whether certain *perceptual judgments* could be significantly altered as a result of participation in a program of movement education. The perceptual attributes explored included the manner in which

---

* For reasonably precise statements concerning the manner in which movement and certain perceptual attributes may or may not be mutually affective, the reader is referred to CRATTY, B. J.: *Perceptual and Motor Development in Infants and Children.* New York, Macmillan, 1970.

geometric figures are related to each other in a drawing task, and the facility with which the children could identify their body's parts, its left-right dimensions and their body's location with respect to other objects.

PROCEDURES

Introduction and Discussion of the Tests Used

During the past ten years a program of movement education has been conducted, first in various facilities in Santa Monica, California, and from 1965 to the present time within the Physical Education Department at UCLA. Frequently during these years tests were given to the children to ascertain whether or not improvement had been elicited.* As is often the case, however, it was difficult to obtain groups of comparable controls with which to compare the scores of the children participating in the program. With the cooperation of the Santa Monica City Schools and the Director of Special Education, Dr. Frank Taylor, however, this became possible during the year 1968-1969, and a comparable group of children designated as "educationally handicapped" were tested and retested in the battery of tests which were utilized.

The battery of tests employed constituted only a portion of the tests given to the children within the UCLA program. This limitation was imposed by the time available and by the limited finances available to the investigators. This modified battery consisted of a six-category test purporting to evaluate control of the larger muscle groups of the body (9), and containing subtests of agility, locomotor ability, ball tracking and catching, ball catching, balance and a test requiring the child to identify his body parts and their left-right dimensions. A second drawing test was also administered. This test required a child to copy the manner in which the tester drew and arranged geometric figures, one at a time, on various corners of a large square which

---

* A summary and detailed description of these tests may be found in CRATTY, B. J., AND MARTIN, M. M.: *Perceptual-Motor Attributes in Children.* Philadelphia, Lea & F., 1969.

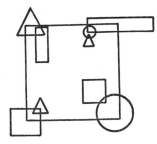

was drawn as the first figure. The completed figure, when drawn properly, looks like this:

Three scores are obtained from this latter test, one reflecting drawing accuracy based upon a 1 to 3 point rating given each figure and then summed; a second score reflecting whether the child located each of the ten figures accurately; and a third score which purportedly tells whether the child drew the figures larger or smaller than the models he was permitted to view.

It is often difficult, of course, to separate the interaction of perceptual and motor factors for proficiency in this test. For example, when the child is asked to copy just this initial part

the child's rendition might be like

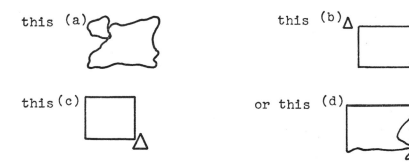

of the figure drawing test, as the experimenter draws first the square and then adds the triangle to one corner like this . . .

Each rendition, of course, probably reflects more than one type of perceptual and/or motor dysfunction. For example, the child submitting a drawing like (a) may be unaware of the differences between his efforts and the model, or he may be aware of the difference. In the former instance, he is thus manifesting inability to guide his hand effectively with his visual apparatus, while in the latter instance he evidences problems in both visually interpreting differences and similarities between geometric figures and in motor deficiency. The drawing (b) might with further evaluation reflect a problem in figure ground perception, as the child resists overlapping figures which, if carried out, might cause him additional problems in separating one figure from the other as he crosses lines. (c) may reflect the inability to correctly organize left-right as well as up-down in space, or the child may not think that it makes any difference. Thus in the former case a real perceptual disturbance may be manifested, while in the latter instance the child's attitude may be interfering with an accurate rendition. (d), of course, suggests that the child is disturbed in a number of ways; it also manifests hand-eye coordination problems.

The battery of gross-motor tests contains an initial section evaluating left-right discrimination as well as identification of body parts and bodily planes (front, side, back, etc.) independent of any left-right judgments. Another portion of the test evaluates what is termed "gross agility" and contains two subtests measuring the facility with which a child can move up and down while remaining within a rather limited amount of space (e.g., how fast can you get up?). The second agility measure combines various locomotor tasks including hopping, jumping and the like; the two subtests include those tests in which the child is asked simply to hop or jump three times in succession while moving forward. It also includes a second subtest in which this type of locomotor activity must be performed with accuracy into small squares within a larger gridded mat. The balance subtest requires the child to maintain various static balances on one foot, with the arms folded, eyes closed and/or on the non-preferred foot to afford added difficulty. The tracking subtest requires the child to catch a playground ball bounced to him and to touch a ball on a string swinging in front of his face, arms' distance away. The throwing test score is based both upon throwing form and upon throwing accuracy. The total possible score in each of the six categories is 10, while the total battery score adds up to 60 points.

Selection and Evaluation of Subjects

The fifty-four children initially tested at UCLA and placed in the experimental group were referred to the program for remediation of motor problems by school psychologists, physicians, teachers and others interested in their welfare. Fourteen of this original group were girls, while the remaining forty were boys. Overall, the children were given neurological examinations and all were described as evidencing various minimal neurological impairments. Their test scores indicated that they were from one to three years behind norms in the tests administered.*

Fifty-seven boys and five girls were tested in classes for the educationally handicapped in the Santa Monica City Schools. These children are generally of average or above average I.Q., but they function academically about two years below norms.

Although it is generally found that there is a greater incidence of children with motor problems in such a population than would be expected in an average classroom, the children selected for this control group were not given neurological examinations, nor were they selected for special training by the Santa Monica City School System because of motor deficits.

When the groups were matched by age and sex, only twenty-eight subjects could be paired in this manner. The final classification for the comparative study was as follows; all of the subjects matched were boys:

Age	Number
(To the nearest birthday)	
7	3
8	6
9	5

---

* These children were also given tests of gender identification, self-concept, drawing and other subjectively scored assessments of skipping, running and the like.

10	6
11	4
12	4
	—
	28

The two groups were tested initially in October and the second testing period was given five months later, in April. During the intervening months the program described in the following section was administered to the experimental subjects. The controls, on the other hand, were afforded no special program of physical education but were merely given recess periods with the usual ball games, swings and climbing apparatus.

Program Description

One of the tenets of "scientific" research concerns its replicability. If a reader is skeptical of the results he should be able to replicate the study to ascertain its veracity. However, the attempt to describe and thus permit the replication of the complexities of a program of education is extremely difficult. If one is to structure the instruction to a marked degree, the teacher cannot accommodate to individual differences in the population of children they deal with. At the same time, in order to accurately describe what is transpiring on a daily basis between teacher and pupil, an incredibly detailed diary must be kept, a methodology which is obviously cumbersome and enormously expensive. Thus the following description of the program to which the experimental group was exposed is of practical necessity composed only of general guidelines rather than exact descriptions. It is hoped that the reader will be tolerant, and yet will obtain a reasonably clear picture of the nature of the educational experiences which were imposed upon the children studied.

The instructors for the program were undergraduate students in psychology, special education and physical education at UCLA. Men students worked with groups of boys, and young women worked with the females in the group. The children were placed in small groups, numbering from three to five children in a group, and were as homogeneous as possible based upon inspection of group profiles of their test scores and upon their ages. The children came to the University for two periods a week, at 3:30 in the afternoon, either on Monday and Wednesday or on Tuesday and Thursday. They remained one hour with their instructors each time. The instructors received one hour of instruction per week from the program administrators, Sister Margaret Mary Martin and Dr. B. J. Cratty. This weekly period was taken up with the introduction and explanation of techniques and/or the discussion of individual children in the various classes.

The instructors were paid for the time during which they worked with the children, as well as for the time they spent in meetings. In addition, the instructors were paid for any time they spent surveying children's records or inspecting instructional materials in times other than regularly scheduled meetings.

Group profiles were given to each instructor so that they might ascertain group strengths and weaknesses. An example of one of these profiles is presented below:

A paperback manual written for parents and teachers was used as a guideline for the program content in order that the instructors could ascertain the general order of difficulty for a child in improving balance and similar attributes (10). Other texts written by the program administrator were also employed,

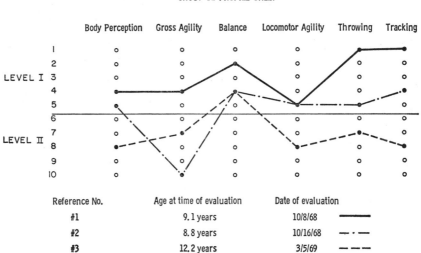

GROUP #2 PROFILE SHEET

including a monograph exploring movement as a learning modality (6), another consisting of game cards (3) and a third explaining how the trampoline might be employed as a developmental tool (4).

During the one-hour period the children were generally in an outdoor facility (lawn, asphalt area) for one-half hour and spent the second part of the hour in an indoor gymnasium. Five small gymnasiums were utilized for this purpose and a large outdoor area and lawn area were also used by the children.

Upon consulting the group profile, an instructor was encouraged to be innovative and to present to the children several types of activities which purportedly would "get at" the attributes in which weakness was measured. Additionally, the children, especially the ones from nine to twelve years of age, were asked what skills they needed especially in order to function well at school (What are you doing on the playground at school? What are you having trouble with when playing?) so that these more specific skills could be enhanced if possible. The child thus would spend about one-half hour working on more basic attributes: balance, agility and the like, and the second one-half hour would be spent on specific sports skills.*

The younger children in the program were afforded fifteen to twenty minutes in the middle of the hour for improvement of manual skills, including practice in drawing geometric figures and in other tasks to improve hand-eye control. The hour would terminate with two activities: a group of four exercises and a time during which the children could be encouraged to "calm down," if needed, prior to being dismissed. Thus a typical hour schedule would look like this:

10 minutes—*agility exercises*: hopping jumping and the like, as well as tumbling exercises on mats.
10 minutes—*balance activities*: using balance beams, static balancing and the like.
10 minutes—*ball skills*: specific instruction in throwing and/or catching balls of various sizes.

---

* The instructors were, for the most part, oblivious to the nature of the test given to the children so that they would not be inclined to "teach towards the test."

10 minutes—*group games*

10 minutes—*trampoline activities*: balance, agility, tricks.

 5 minutes—*strength exercises*: back extensions, pulling exercises of some type, bent knee sit-ups, as well as some kind of pushing exercise for the arms and chest.

 5 minutes—*relaxation training*: impulse control training or similar technique.

When possible, individual differences were accommodated as outlined in the text by Cratty and Martin (5). For example, if a group was extremely hyperactive, the following program might be utilized during the one-hour period:

10 minutes of relaxation training.

10 minutes of agility and balance activities.

10 minutes of ball handling skills.

10 minutes of trampoline activities.

 5 minutes of exercises.

15 minutes of additional practice in impulse control and relaxation training.

The instructors, as the five-month experimental period progressed, were thus given general guidelines to follow: sequences of motor tasks in order of difficulty, group profiles of the children in their charge and general advice on how to accommodate to individual differences.

The experiences afforded the children constituted both those which attempted to improve basic perceptual-motor attributes in which the children evidenced deficiencies and those which attempted to improve specific sports skills which enabled the children to function better within the social situations on the playground which confronted them at school.

Analysis of the Data

The data were analyzed in the following manner. Initially, independent group comparisons were made between the total number children tested within each of the sites (UCLA and Santa Monica), comparing total motor and drawing test scores obtained prior to and at the completion of the five-month training period. Additionally, comparisons of change in the various scores obtained were made using the twenty-eight children in each of the two matched groups at both sites. These latter scores were analyzed and compared by subtest as well as by age.

Summary of Procedures

Pre- and posttest comparisons were made of twenty-eight children in two groups, an experimental and control, employing a battery of motor tests together with a figure drawing test. The five-month program of movement education afforded the experimental group consisted of two-a-week classes, one hour in duration, in which the experimental subjects were given activities purporting to enhance various perceptual-motor competencies in which they had exhibited weaknesses. Pre- and posttest differences were analyzed within each population. On the six-category test of gross motor ability the mean was 47.84 prior to the five-month period (S.D. 5.91) while the posttest mean was 49.79 (S.D. .96). There was a significant change in the overall motor ability as measured by this test in the total Santa Monica group ($t = 3.23$, significant at the 1% level) (pre- and posttest $r = .78$).

Drawing Scores of the Total Groups Tested

The total drawing score was compiled by summing the score elicited from assessing location of figures and from the total accuracy score. The pretest mean of this total drawing score by the original group of fifty-four children tested in the UCLA group was 14.81 (S.D. 8.34), while the posttest mean of the total group was 17.47 (S.D. 8.02). The t of 4.33 computed indicated that a significant change had occurred in the children's ability to accurately draw the figure test and in the ability to place the figures in proper relationship to each other. The two scores obtained from the total group were remarkably consistent, as the pre- and posttest correlation was .85.

A similar positive change was not elicited in the total Santa Monica group, as the pretest mean was 19.00 (S.D. 4.71) and the posttest mean was 18.65 (S.D. 4.66). The t = .67 and pre- and posttest correlation of the total score was .74.

Intergroup Comparisons of Total Group Scores

Comparisons of the means of the gross motor ability test and the drawing test clearly established the fact that the total Santa Monica group was significantly superior to the total UCLA group tested in both types of attributes. For example, the pretest mean scores of the total Santa Monica group in the gross motor battery was 47.84 (S.D. 5.91), as compared to the UCLA group mean of only 38.64 (S.D. 8.75; t = 8.83 significant exceeding the 1% level). The comparison of the drawing score revealed similar differences in favor of the Santa Monica group, as their pretest drawing mean was 19.00 (S.D. 4.71), as compared to the UCLA group mean of 14.81 (S.D. 8.34; t = 4.32, significant at the 1% level). It can also be seen upon comparison of the standard deviations that the UCLA group's drawing scores were significantly more variable than were those obtained from the Santa Monica controls.

To summarize, the intergroup comparisons of the pre- and posttest scores based upon the responses of the total subjects tested prior to matching groups revealed the following:

1. Both the UCLA and Santa Monica groups improved significantly in tests of gross motor ability over the five-month period. The UCLA group registered a mean improvement of 5.19 points on this test, while the Santa Monica group's mean improvement was 1.95 points.
2. The total UCLA group improved significantly in the drawing test (of accuracy and location of figures), while the total Santa Monica group did not.
3. Remarkably consistent scores were obtained on the two groups when pre- and posttest scores were correlated. These r's ranged from +.74 to +.85.
4. The total UCLA group was inferior to the total Santa Monica group in the test of gross motor ability and in the drawing test.

Comparisons of Matched Groups

Twenty-eight boys from each group were matched by age in order to carry out more valid comparisons between the scores elicited from the controls and from the experimental subjects.

The age breakdown may be found in the preceding; the mean age was 9.54 for the Santa Monica group (S.D. 1.56) and 9.23 for the UCLA group (S.D. 1.35). Thus there was no significant difference between the mean age of the groups (t = .13).

TABLE XXXI

COMPARISON OF PRE- AND POSTTEST MEAN SCORES FOR THE MATCHED EXPERIMENTAL AND CONTROL GROUPS

Gross Motor Battery		Pretest (N = 28)			Posttest (N = 28)		
		UCLA	SM	t	UCLA	SM	t
1. Body percept.	M	8.07	8.75	1.36	8.78	8.60	0.39
	S.D.	2.20	1.40		1.80	1.56	
2. Gross agility	M	8.25	8.67	0.94	8.89	8.39	1.04
	S.D.	1.97	1.23		1.52	1.97	
3. Balance	M	5.96	8.14	4.75*	7.21	8.17	1.66
	S.D.	1.78	1.60		2.11	2.14	
4. Locomotor	M	6.64	7.82	2.55	8.35	8.85	1.27
	S.D.	1.61	1.79		1.54	1.35	
5. Throwing	M	4.96	6.10	1.87	5.78	6.00	0.36
	S.D.	2.07	2.41		2.16	2.26	
6. Tracking	M	6.96	8.21	2.35	7.71	8.35	1.15
	S.D.	2.30	1.54		2.50	1.44	
Total	M	40.85	47.64		46.75	48.42	
	S.D.	7.75	6.78	3.42*	8.59	6.36	0.81
Figure Drawing Test							
Size	M	1.64	1.07	0.09	1.71	1.00	0.03
	S.D.	0.55	0.25		0.58	00	
Accuracy	M	10.42	9.14	1.33	10.75	8.89	1.93
	S.D.	3.56	3.48		3.49	3.59	
Location	M	6.35	8.35	3.36*	7.82	8.64	1.56
	S.D.	2.75	1.42		2.43	1.26	

* Differences significant at 5 percent level.

As can be seen from Table XXXI, comparing the mean pretest scores of the matched group, the Santa Monica controls were superior in most of the tests administered prior to the initiation of the educational program on the part of the experimentals at UCLA. However, as can also be seen following the testing after the five-month period of participation in the program of movement education, the superiority of the Santa Monica group tended to disappear. Whereas, prior to training the Santa Monica controls were significantly superior in the balance score (t = 4.75), in the total battery score (t = 3.42) significant differences were almost achieved in the scores evaluating tracking and locomotor agility by the end of the training program. The Santa Monica controls were not superior on any of these measures of gross motor ability.

Similarly, it can be seen, upon inspection of Table XXXI, that the UCLA group also "caught up" with the Santa Monica group in the ability to locate figures properly on the drawing test. Prior to training, the UCLA group was significantly inferior to the Santa Monica group in this respect and was able on the average to locate only about six out of ten correctly. After training for five months, the average score of the UCLA experimental group indicated that almost eight out of ten were located correctly on the complex figure drawing test.

Table XXXII illustrates the amount of change elicited in the controls following training. As can be seen in the score obtained from the UCLA controls, significant change was elicited in the gross motor battery score and in subtests evaluating balance and locomotor agility. Also, significant changes were elicited in the location subscore of the figure drawing test. No significant changes were noted when the mean scores of the subtests evaluating body perception, gross agility, throwing and tracking were contrasted. It should be noted, however, that the mean scores on the pretest for gross agility, body perception and tracking equal norms for these tests (5).

As can also be seen from inspection of Table XXXII, remarkably consistent pre- and posttest scores were elicited in tests evaluating location of figures on the drawing test (r = .72) and in the total drawing test (r = .81), and on the subtests of the gross motor ability battery evaluating balance (r = .68), despite the fact that a five-month interval separated the two administrations of the test.

Survey of the Scores of the Santa Monica Controls

As can be seen from Table XXXIII, no significant improvement was seen in the mean scores in any of the tests by the controls. It should also be noted, however, that in some cases their initial mean scores are closer to the norms than was true within the experimental group. For example, in the subtests evaluating body perception, balance and tracking the Santa

TABLE XXXII

COMPARISON OF PRE- AND POSTTEST SCORES COLLECTED
FROM THE UCLA CONTROLS

Gross Motor Test (N = 28)		*Pretest*	*Posttest*	*t*	*r*
1. Body percept.	M	8.07	8.78	1.60	.36
	S.D.	2.20	1.80		
2. Gross agility	M	8.25	8.89	1.70	.40
	S.D.	1.97	1.52		
3. Balance	M	5.96	7.21	4.08*	.68
	S.D.	1.78	2.11		
4. Locomotor agility	M	6.64	8.35	5.46*	.47
	S.D.	1.61	1.54		
5. Throwing	M	4.96	5.78	2.39	.65
	S.D.	2.07	2.16		
6. Tracking	M	6.96	7.71	1.46	.39
	S.D.	2.30	2.50		
Total	M	40.85	46.75	4.65*	.68
	S.D.	7.75	8.59		
Drawing					
Size	M	1.64	1.71	0.61	.46
	S.D.	.55	.58		
Accuracy	M	10.42	10.75	0.63	.71
	S.D.	3.56	3.49		
Location	M	6.35	7.82	3.88*	.72
	S.D.	2.75	2.43		
Total	M	18.42	20.25	2.62	.81
	S.D.	6.03	5.60		

* Differences significant at 5 percent level.

Monica group was already performing at levels expected for groups of children with a mean age of 9.5 years. However, for the subtests purporting to evaluate locomotor ability, throwing and gross agility, the Santa Monica group was below norms and with no special training did not evidence improvement over the five-month period of time.

Comparisons of Change as a Function of Age

A survey of pre- and posttest mean scores, in both the experimental (UCLA) and control (Santa Monica) groups was made within several age categories. This survey did not involve any formal statistical treatment of the data, due to the small number of subjects within each age category. The results of this survey, however, reveals that in general the most marked improvement can apparently be elicited on the part of the younger children within the experimental group. For example, the mean score changes in the gross motor battery at age seven in the UCLA

TABLE XXXIII

COMPARISON OF PRE- AND POSTTEST SCORES COLLECTED
FROM THE SANTA MONICA CONTROLS

Gross Motor Battery (N = 28)		Pretest	Posttest	t	r
1. Body percept.	M	8.75	8.60	0.47	.41
	S.D.	1.40	1.56		
2. Gross agility	M	8.67	8.39	0.95	.64
	S.D.	1.23	1.97		
3. Balance	M	8.14	8.17	0.12	.81
	S.D.	1.60	2.14		
4. Locomotor agility	M	7.82	8.85	2.66	.21
	S.D.	1.79	1.35		
5. Throwing	M	6.10	6.00	0.24	.58
	S.D.	2.41	2.26		
6. Tracking	M	8.21	8.35	0.57	.65
	S.D.	1.54	1.44		
Total	M	47.64	48.42	1.15	.86
	S.D.	6.78	6.36		
Drawing Test					
Size	M	1.07	1.00		
	S.D.	0.25	.00		
Accuracy	M	9.14	8.89	0.51	.75
	S.D.	3.48	3.59		
Location	M	8.35	8.36	1.38	.69
	S.D.	1.42	1.26		
Total	M	18.57	18.53	0.076	.81
	S.D.	4.40	4.32		

group was 7.34 points, at age eight it was 10 points, and at age nine it was 10.2 points. However, following that age the experimentals evidenced little overall improvement in the scores reflecting gross motor ability (i.e. at ten years improvement was only 1.37 points, at eleven years improvement was 2.75 points, and age twelve improvement was on the average only 3.50 points). Thus almost three times more improvement in mean scores was recorded in the children (N-14) of nine years of age and under than was recorded in the mean scores of fourteen children ten years of age and older.

As would be expected, the changes by age were negligible in the controls; at age seven mean change was only 1 point, 3 points' difference at age eight, the nine-year-olds from Santa Monica evidenced a mean change in the gross motor ability test of only 3 points, no improvement was seen in the mean scores of the ten year olds, and only 1 point was seen in the mean score change of the eleven and twelve-year-olds.

TABLE XXXIV

COMPARISON OF MEAN SCORES ON THE GROSS MOTOR ABILITY TEST
BY AGE WITHIN THE TWO MATCHED GROUPS*

Santa Monica Controls ($N = 28$)

Age	7(N=3)	8(N=6)	9(N=5)	10(N=6)	11(N=4)	12(N=4)
Pretest mean	43	43	44	54	49	49
Posttest mean	42	46	46	54	48	50

UCLA Experimentals ($N = 28$)

Age	7(N=3)	8(N=6)	9(N=5)	10(N=6)	11(N=4)	12(N=4)
Pretest mean	40	34	40	39	44	49
Posttest mean	48	44	51	40	47	52

* Scores rounded off to the nearest whole number.

This diminishing improvement as a function of age is probably due to the nature of the testing instrument.

As one approaches the upper limits of any test it becomes more difficult to register improvement. At the same time, however, it may be that the older children's motor abilities, whether good or bad, became relatively fixed after passing middle childhood. A more thorough discussion of this finding may be found in the section which follows.

Summary of the Findings

A survey of the findings revealed the following:

1. The total of fifty-four subjects tested twice at UCLA, separated by a five-month training period, evidenced significant improvement of 5.19 points in the ability to perform on a battery of gross motor tests and in the "location" subscore of the drawing test.

2. The total of forty-four children in Santa Monica (controls) similarly evidenced a significant mean change of 1.95 points in the total gross motor test battery, but showed no improvement in the drawing test nor in any of the subscores reflecting proficiency in this latter task.

3. Consistent pre- and posttest scores were elicited from the two groups when the two scores were correlated (r's ranged from +.74 to +.85).

4. The total Santa Monica group (N=44) were superior in motor ability and in drawing competence to the total UCLA group (N=53).

5. Matched group comparisons (N=28 in each group) re-

vealed that the Santa Monica controls possessed significantly better motor ability initially than did the UCLA experimentals.

6. Following the five-month training period the Santa Monica controls were not superior to the UCLA controls in any of the subtest scores in tests of motor ability and drawing.

7. Following these experimental periods the UCLA subjects evidenced significant change in gross motor ability, in the subtests reflecting proficiency in locating figures on the drawing test and in balance and locomotor agility.

8. Following the experimental period no significant changes were found in the mean scores of any of the subtests on the part of the control subjects (N=28) in Santa Monica.

9. Comparisons of change elicited as a function of age revealed that almost three times as much change was elicited in subjects within the experimental group between the ages of seven and nine than was seen in the mean scores of subjects within this same group who were ten to twelve years of age. No significant changes were seen within the control group as a function of age.

10. Correlation of pre- and posttest scores within the matched samples again revealed reasonably consistent performance on the part of the two populations.

CONCLUSIONS AND DISCUSSION
OF THE FINDINGS

Upon surveying the data it is apparent that significant changes can be elicited in basic motor and selected perceptual attributes of children with moderate motor problems within a five-month period of time.

A thorough analysis of the data, as well as a consideration of some of the subjective information obtained as a result of this research program, revealed several weaknesses within the present study. For example, it is doubtful that the Santa Monica group represented true controls, insofar as they had been selected by the Santa Monica City Schools as children evidencing educational rather than motor problems. While on many of the subtests of motor control—as would be expected in such a group—

their mean scores were below norms, our controls, as a group, did not evidence the same degree of motor ineptitude as did the children with the experimental group who sought a program of remediation specifically designed to correct movement ineptitude.

It is believed that to correctly apply programs of movement education to populations of children who have evidenced educational difficulties, two basic premises must be adhered to: (a) It must not be assumed that all such children will evidence coordination problems. (b) This group of children must be carefully screened to separate those who evidence movement deficiencies from those who do not, with separate and more basic programs of remediation planned for the former subgroup.

It was similarly interesting to note the change in the manner in which the children within the experimental group located figures relative to each other in the drawing task. While this group did not evidence any significant improvement in drawing accuracy, neither was a concomitant change noted in the controls. These data, it is believed, hold several implications for individuals planning programs which purport to improve drawing and writing competence in children who have been identified as evidencing motor and/or educational difficulties. It seems apparent that a program of movement tasks in which up-down and left-right are emphasized may exert a significant improvement in the rather global perceptions needed to locate figures (and thus perhaps letters in words, words in sentences, the left and right of sentences?) in space; but at the same time, if it is desired to aid children to improve their accuracy of the hand-eye coordinations needed when drawing, specific help in this type of task is needed. Moreover, these data and those from previous studies indicate that the following principles are valid ones with respect to the ways in which children can be aided in the structuring of space in rather global ways:

(a) The left-right and up-down, etc. of the child's body can be learned through engaging in various movement tasks, but unless in direct ways the child is taught that space has these same dimensions ("See, the 'd' faces toward your left hand," etc.), little transfer between perceptions about the left-right of the body and the left-right of space will likely occur.

(b) Improvement in drawing accuracy will only come about through specific training in tasks requiring accurate hand-eye movements. Little or no transfer may be expected between improvement in gross motor attributes and fine motor skill.

The data also revealed that improvement in motor attributes more basic than sports skills are possible through participation in various tasks without specific training toward the tests themselves. For example, it appears that participation in several types of balance tasks both static and dynamic (beam walking, etc.) can elicit significant change in a test of static balance which is not specifically trained for. Vincent (23) has found that transfer occurred between tasks of seated and standing balance. Further research might reveal that transfer between training in static and dynamic balance might be elicited.

It is believed that the data also revealed that relatively brief training sessions, lasting only a total of two hours a week, can exert significant change in motor attributes on the part of children with movement problems. The estimates of the incidence of this type of problem within purportedly "normal" populations of children ranges between 5 and 18.2 percent according to recent studies. Hopefully, studies of the type carried out here will encourage school personnel to take two important steps toward the remediation of problems of this type among a large percent of the children entering school. Initially, and early in their school career (the day the child first enters school would be appropriate) the child should be given a screening test composed either of tasks which approximately 80 percent of all children of that age and sex could be expected to perform, or of tasks which elicit a numerical score on a continuum. From the results of this screening test, two further steps should be taken:

(a) The children thus identified should be given more thorough evaluations designed to uncover neurological motor and perceptual deficiencies in a more definitive manner.

(b) Planned programs of remediation should be undertaken in the schools, consisting of special classes in which basic motor activities designed to improve both fine and gross motor control might be placed. It has been demonstrated in this study that two one-hour periods a week can exert significant change in gross motor abilities and in certain perceptual attributes (i.e. locating figures properly in space). It would appear that three periods of from thirty to forty-five minutes each, spaced throughout the school week, might prove even more helpful and would elicit even more improvement than was demonstrated here.

One of the most important findings within the data, however, concerns the differences in improvement evidenced in early childhood (7 to 9 years) versus the improvement seen in children in later childhood (10 to 12 years). The more marked improvement seen in the younger age group gives weight to the postulate of Benjamin Bloom stated in the text titled *Stability and Change in Human Characteristics* (1). He suggests that the amount of change which may be elicited through education in a given attribute or set of attributes at a given time in a child's life is dependent upon the amount of change which would be expected to occur by chance during the same period of the child's adolescent life. Thus political attitudes may be more likely to be changed between the years of eighteen to twenty, while changes in motor abilities are more likely to be modifiable in the early years of life, during which time they are normally in a state of flux. It is probable that even more marked change could be demonstrated in the attributes scrutinized in this investigation in an even younger population of children than was seen in the children from seven to nine years of age.

This type of finding, of course, has important implications for school personnel. To identify and to remediate perceptual-motor problems in children as they first enter the first grade or nursery school would seem to be more expedient than waiting until the child's movement behavior and attitudes about his motor attributes become fixed in later childhood.

The findings of this investigation thus coincide with those from studies by Singer, Johnson and others (15, 21, 22). That is, significant improvement in basic motor ability traits of children can be accomplished with the institution of reasonable and regularly practiced programs of remediation. It is hoped that school personnel heed these findings and similar results from other investigations and invest time and money in developmental screenings early in the child's school career, and then institute programs of remediation for those children found to be deficient.

BIBLIOGRAPHY

1. BLOOM, BENJAMIN S.: *Stability and Change in Human Characteristics,* New York, Wiley, 1966.
2. BROWN, ROSCOE C.: The effect of a perceptual-motor education program on perceptual-motor skills and reading readiness. Presented at Research Section, AAHPER, St. Louis, Missouri, April 1, 1968.
3. CRATTY, BRYANT J.: *Moving and Learning: Fifty Games for Children with Learning Difficulties.* Freeport, Long Island, Educational Activities, Inc., 1968.
4. CRATTY, BRYANT J.: *Trampoline Activities for Atypical Children.* Palo Alto, Peek Publications, 1969.
5. CRATTY, BRYANT J., AND MARTIN, MARGARET MARY: *Perceptual-Motor Efficiency in Children, The Measurement and Improvement of Movement Attributes.* Philadelphia: Lea & F., 1969.
6. CRATTY, BRYANT J.: *Movement, Perception and Thought.* Palo Alto, Peek Publications, 1969.
7. CRATTY, BRYANT J.: *Movement Behavior and Motor Learning,* 3rd ed. Philadelphia, Lea & F., 1967.
8. CRATTY, BRYANT J.: *Perceptual and Motor Development in Children.* New York, Macmillan, 1970.
9. CRATTY, BRYANT J.: *Perceptual-Motor Behavior and Educational Processes.* Springfield, Thomas, 1969.
10. CRATTY, BRYANT J.: *Developmental Sequences of Perceptual-Motor Tasks for Neurologically Handicapped and Retarded Children.* Freeport, Long Island, Educational Activities, 1967.
11. DUNNING, JACK D., AND KEPHART, N. C.: Motor generalization in space and time. In Hellmuth, Jerome (Ed.): *Learning Disorders,* Vol. I. Seattle, Special Child, 1965.

12. FLEISHMAN, EDWIN A.: *The Structure and Measurement of Physical Fitness.* Englewood Cliffs, New Jersey, Prentice-Hall, 1964.

13. GEARHEART, BILL R.: A study of a physical education program designed to promote motor skills of educable mentally retarded children enrolled in special education classes in Cedar Rapids, Iowa. Research Study No. 1, Dissertation Abstracts 25 (1), 271-272.

14. HILL, S. D.; McCULLUM, A. H., AND SCEAU, H.: Relation of training in motor activity to development of left-right directionality in mentally retarded children: exploratory study. *Percept Motor Skills,* 24:363-366, 1967.

15. JOHNSON, WARREN R., AND FRITZ, BRUCE R.: Changes in perceptual motor skills after a chlidren's physical development program. *Percept Motor Skills,* 24:610, 1967.

16. KEPHART, NEWELL C.: *The Slower Learner in the Classroom.* Columbus, Ohio, Merrill, C. E., 1960.

17. KERSHNER, JOHN R.: Doman-Delacato's theory of neurological organization applied with retarded children. *Exceptional Child.* 33:441-450, 1968.

18. LaPRAY, MARGARET, AND ROSS, RAMON: Auditory and visual-perceptual training. In Figurel, J. Allen (Ed.): *Vistas in Reading.* International Reading Association Conference Proceedings, XI, 1966, 530-532.

19. ROACH, EUGENE G.: Evaluation of an experimental program of perceptual-motor training with slow readers. In Figurel, J. Allen (Ed.): *Vistas in Reading.* International Reading Association Conference Proceedings, XI, 1966, 446-450.

20. RUTHERFORD, WILLIAM L.: Perceptual-motor training and readiness. In Figurel, J. Allen (Ed.): *Reading and Inquiry.* International Reading Association Conference Proceedings, X, 1965, 194-196.

21. SINGER, ROBERT N., AND BRINK, J. W.: Relation of perceptual-motor ability and intellectual ability in elementary school children. *Percept Motor Skills,* 24:967-970, 1967.

22. SOLOMON, A., AND PRANGLE, R.: Demonstrations of physical fitness improvement in the EMR. *Exceptional Child,* 33:177-181, 1967.

23. VINCENT, WILLIAM J.: *Transfer Effects Between Motor Skills Judged Similar in Perceptual Components.* Unpublished Doctoral Dissertation, University of California, Los Angeles, 1966.

Chapter IV

TOTAL BODY MOVEMENT AS A LEARNING MODALITY, A PILOT STUDY*

INTRODUCTION AND PURPOSE

Movement and manipulative experiences have long been employed in programs for the retarded. In Rome around the turn of the century, Maria Montessori employed tactual tasks (17). More recently, various movement experiences have been advanced by Fernald (22), Delacato (12), Barsch (4), Kephart (15), Getman (12) and others for the improvement of children with learning difficulties. The effectiveness of various programs of physical education have been studied by Oliver (18), Corder (6), Solomon and Prangle (24), Rarick and Broadhead (19) and others (16, 21). James Humphrey has investigated the way in which games contribute to the manner whereby normal children acquire arithmetic skills and language skills (14).

Using program content as a criterion, these regimes may be classified as follows:

1. Those containing traditional physical education activities, games, exercises and the like—Corder (6), Oliver (17), Solomon and Prangle (24), and Humphrey (14).
2. Programs involving highly structured gross motor activity —Delacato (12), Kershner (16), Robbins (21), Yarborough (25), Kephart (15), Brown (5), Rutherford (23) and Anderson (3).
3. Tactual-manipulative activity—Montessori (16), and Fernald (22).

---

* The pilot study which follows was administered and taught by Sister Margaret Mary Martin, M.S. from January, 1969 to June, 1969.

Theoretically the programs outlined above may be classified as follows:

1. Some are based upon a central cognitive theory—i.e., movement activities which provoke thought may improve intelligence—Humphrey (14), Rarick and Broadhead (19), Cratty (7, 8, 9, 11).
2. Others are based upon a "dynamic" theory—i.e., improvement in academic and intellectual processes will be derived indirectly, as motivating and successful experiences in play are realized by children, which will in turn heighten self-concept and a willingness to "try harder" at academic as well as at motor tasks (18).
3. Programs based upon some theory of perceptual training through movement constitute another type—i.e. all learning stems from motor functioning, which contributes to perceptual development, which in turn forms the basis of intelligence—Getman (13), Kephart (15) and Barsch (4).
4. A theory of cortical integration is also found in the literature—i.e., movement activities at various developmental levels will somehow improve the functioning of various parts of the central nervous system, which in turn will positively influence other peripheral processes (vision, audition, etc.) purportedly mediated by the same portions of the brain which control the motor functions practiced (12).

In general, recent research evidence fails to support the validity of the various theories of perceptual-motor training. For example, in studies by Roach (20) and Brown (5) no significant differences in academic achievement and in reading were evidenced by experimental groups exposed to this type of program.

At the same time, recent research similarly suggests that the validity of the central theory of neural-motor integration espoused by Delacato is questionable. Robbins (21), Anderson (3) and Yarborough (25), for example, all failed to find any appreciable gain in intelligence, reading or in perceptual functioning on the part of children who participated in a program of cross-pattern creeping and crawling. As a result of this research the methodology has been widely condemned by professional groups in the United States and elsewhere (1, 2). The study by Kershner which presents positive findings contains several questionable conclusions.*

Research during the past ten years is only partially supportive of a "dynamic theory" of motivation relative to improvement of academic and intellectual functions through movement. Although the findings by Oliver in 1958 (18), and later by Corder (6), suggest that gains in I.Q. scores are recorded after retarded children are exposed to traditional programs of physical education games and fitness exercises, in a later and more carefully controlled study by Solomon and Prangle (24) it was found that, in general, traditional motor activities applied to retardates will result in the improvement of motor functions while little gain in I.Q. may be expected.*

Recent findings, it is believed, are more supportive of a central-cognitive theory of learning through movement. For example, the study by Rarick and Broadhead (19) utilized a physical education program in which the retarded children were given "movement problems" to think about. It was found that following this type of program of activities, significantly positive gains in I.Q. scores measured by the Peabody Picture Test were achieved by their experimental group. Using normal children Humphrey similarly found that when games were used to teach arithmetic and language skills, more improvement was realized

---

* His controls improved more than his experimentals in an extensive battery of perceptual-motor tests and it was concluded that while the Delacato method was not supported with this finding, that the Kephart theory was. This kind of *post hoc* hypothesis formation is of dubious scientific merit.

* Oliver correctly reasoned, it is believed, that the children he tested in England improved in I.Q. because of a heightened self-concept. When the Hawthorne effect of instructor rapport is controlled for, as in the investigation by Solomon and Prangle, and activities are taught without opportunities for the participating children to engage in decisions about their program, little change in intelligence can be expected, despite gains in muscle size, fitness levels and the like.

than was attained by his classroom controls who studied the usual workbooks on these same subjects (14).

Thus, it is believed that as current research findings suggest, retarded children may be taught to think more efficiently through movement to the extent to which they are encouraged to think about the movement activities they engage in.

Despite the apparent validity of the above statement, however, it is often difficult to know just how to encourage retarded children to think when moving or prior to performing a motor task. Additionally, it is often more difficult to determine just *what* a retarded child should or can think about prior to engaging in various physical activities.

With these goals in mind it has been attempted within the past several years in the Perceptual-Motor Learning Laboratory at the University of California, Los Angeles, to devise programs incorporating movement experiences which will aid retardates to acquire certain academic and cognitive skills.

The pilot study to be reported had two primary purposes. First, it was purposed to establish testing procedures which would provide valid and reliable indices of selected academic operations (spelling, serial memory ability, pattern and letter recognition, etc.). Second, it was purposed to determine whether any significant change in these characteristics would occur following a program of learning experiences which incorporated activities requiring movement of the total body.

As the investigation incorporated no control groups, conclusions arrived at may only be inferential rather than positive. It is believed, however, that conclusions would be more positive with the introduction of a group controlling for the "Hawthorne Effect" (i.e., engaging in recreational activities), a group controlling for the perceptual training involved (i.e., learning in small groups while seated at desks), and, of course, a group in which no type of activities would be introduced, and which would only be administered tests before and after the training period to which the other groups would be exposed. A more elaborate study of this nature, incorporating proper controls, is being utilized for the school year 1969-1970.

INITIAL PROCEDURES

An Overview

Preliminary procedures included contacting the administrators of Elementary Education for the Catholic Archdiocese of Los Angeles for permission to investigate the effects of the pilot-study program over a period of about six weeks. After this initial period of time, eight children whose progress was "lagging" (a series of screening tests were administered informally at this point), were also given extra individual help. These eight participated in extra one-half hour sessions on Tuesday and Thursday mornings in addition to the regular classes.

At the end of a period of five months the twenty-nine children were again tested on the battery of tests. Inspection of pre- and posttest data, as well as observations made while the instructional program was being conducted, formed a basis for recommendations pertinent to the improvement of the testing and instructional program.

School Selection and Identification of Subjects

The Catholic Archdiocese of Los Angeles administers approximately 263 elementary schools. Many of these schools serve children who might be described as culturally and or economically deprived. The selected school, St. Malachy's, is located in South Central Los Angeles slightly north of the Watts area. Its population consists of about 90 percent Negro and 10 percent who have Spanish surnames and who will be considered as Mexican-American. The median income for the families of the children attending St. Malachy's is from $3,000 to $4,500 per year. Although the tuition charged is $10 per month, most of the children pay less and many are not charged anything for their education. The school has a well-stocked library and a large asphalt playground. The facilities for conducting the program incorporated into this investigation were located in a large combination auditorium-cafeteria (size 45' x 35').

The twenty-nine children selected for participation in the investigation were taken from the first through the fourth grades. The age range was from six to ten years, with a mean age of 7.73 (S.D. 1.19).

The children selected met the following criteria:

1. They were initially identified by their teachers as having academic difficulties including problems in learning to read, spell and giving their attention to classroom work.
2. Their I.Q. was 80 or below on the vocabulary section of the Gray Oral Reading Test.
3. They fell into the "low" category of the Metropolitan Reading Readiness Test, Form A.

Overall, the following chart summarizes the children of each sex, selected from each grade, 1 through 4.

Grade	Males	Females	Total
1	5	6	11
2	6	0	6
3	4	3	7
4	1	4	5
Total	16	13	29

One fourth-grade girl, one second-grade boy and one third-grade boy had Spanish surnames, the remainder of the children were Negroes.

Preliminary Testing

Twice within two consecutive days tests with six categories were administered to fifteen of the children. These tests consisted of tasks to evaluate:

1. *Persistence (3 subtests)*

   WALKING PERSISTENCE

   A score was obtained by determining how long it would take a child to "walk around the square" (4' x 4'). The score was timed to the nearest tenth of a second and the child was stopped after three minutes if he continued that long.

   PERSISTENCE TO PICTURE BOOK

   The time during which a child was willing to look at a picture book, *Classroom Cartoons for all Occasions* (Jerome C. Brown), was clocked to the nearest tenth of a second.

   PERSISTENCE AT BALL CATCHING

   The examiner, using a regulation playground ball (8½"

in diameter), and standing ten feet away, bounced a ball to the child to determine whether he would remain attentive to the task (i.e., continue to return it). The test was stopped if the child reached twenty catches and returns. The score was recorded in terms of the number of catches and returns the child engaged in before he stopped.

2. *Perceptual-Motor Abilities (4 subtests)*

The test purporting to evaluate balance, gross agility, locomotor agility and body perception (Levels I and II) from a battery employed in previous investigations by Cratty and Martin (11).

3. *Pattern Recognition (2 subtests)*

VISUAL IDENTIFICATION OF PATTERNS

Cards (5" x 8") were held up one at a time for two seconds in front of the child. Each card contained one geometric figure (triangle, circle, square, rectangle, half-circle and diamond). The child was required to select and to point to the corresponding figure on a dittoed sheet containing all of the figures which were placed in front of him. The child was required to make his identification after the experimenter removed the stimulus figure. The score obtained was the number of correct responses; the maximum score possible was 6.

VERBAL IDENTIFICATION OF FIGURES

The procedures were the same as above except that the child was required to verbally identify the stimulus figures after they were presented one at a time. Scoring was carried out in the same way.

4. *Letter Recognition (2 subtests)*

VERBAL RESPONSE

Block printed (uppercase) letters were randomly presented one at a time on 5" x 8" cards for a two-second interval. Following presentation the card was placed face down on the table and the child was required to name the letter just exposed. One point was given if the correct response was given within two seconds following presentation. The total possible score was 26.

WRITTEN RESPONSE

Twenty-six printed lowercase letters were presented in the same manner as above, but in this test the child was required to write the letter within two seconds after each one was removed from his view. One point was scored for each correctly reproduced letter, and the maximum possible was 26.

5. *Serial Memory Ability* (*2 subtests*)

MEMORY FOR PICTURES

Six pictures of animals (dog, cat, bird, fish, horse, elephant) were presented to the child. First a single picture, then two, then three, etc., until all six were presented. Between each presentation the child was required to repeat the names of the animals in correct order. The total possible score (all responses on all presentations) was 21.

MEMORY FOR GESTURES

Six gestures were made by the experimenter in the same manner as above, i.e., "building up" from one, then two, then three, etc., until a total of six were seen. The child standing six feet away was required to imitate them in correct order and was afforded two seconds to complete each gesture. The gestures consisted of arm positions (i.e., arms folded, arms up, bent arms, etc.) as well as positions in which the hands touched various body parts (hands on shoulders, on top of head, touching ears, etc.). The total possible score or the total correct responses on all presentations was 21.

6. *Spelling*

Using twenty words from the Dolch Basic Word List and from the Stanford Achievement Tests for Primary I, the child was dictated each word at two second intervals and was permitted two seconds to begin to write or print the word. The first-grade children were not given this test.

Analysis of the Data From Preliminary Testing

Rank order correlations were computed using fifteen subjects' scores between test and retest results as well as between selected subtest scores obtained in the initial testing session.

Using scores from retarded children, the subtests from the Cratty Battery of Perceptual-Motor Tests were found to be reliable in previous investigations and thus were not contrasted in this preliminary study (10).

In general the test-retest r's obtained from the tests of persistence were not high enough to justify their further use. Persistence in walking the square was not significant (r = .24), while persistence in ball bouncing was not computed as all but two of the children were content to remain with the tester for all twenty bounces, and the scores derived from clocking the duration of attention to the picture book on two trials was .68.

The reliability of the other tests met acceptable standards, with the exception of the verbal response to patterns and the serial memory tests, but it was hoped that with certain changes in the administration of these plus the addition of more subjects, reliability coefficients might become higher. Summarized, the correlations between test-retest scores in the various tests administered during this preliminary testing period are as follows:

Selected correlations computed (rank order) between the various tests revealed that significant (at the 5% level) relation-

Test	*r*
CRATTY BATTERY	
Body Perception	.82
Gross Agility	.82
Locomotor Agility	.84
Balance	.80
PERSISTENCE	
Square Walking	.24
Ball Bouncing	not computed
Picture Book	.68
PATTERN RECOGNITION	
Verbal Response	.89
Visual Recognition	.64
LETTER RECOGNITION	
Verbal (upper-case)	.98
Written (lower-case)	.93
SERIAL MEMORY	
Pictures	.79
Gestures	.73
SPELLING	.96

ships existed between the various scores obtained. For example, there was a +.58 correlation between the scores obtained from the test of visual recognition of patterns and the scores elicited from the body perception category. Similarly, there were a number of significant r's obtained when the scores reflecting proficiency in visual recognition of patterns were contrasted to other scores obtained (i.e. +.50 with verbal identification of patterns, +.54 with verbal identification of letters, +.79 with written identification of letters, +.64 with serial memory of pictures, +.53 with serial memory of gestures and +.59 with the spelling score). The data thus indicate the fact that pattern recognition may underlie the learning of a rather large number of schoolroom tasks.

There were other significant correlations obtained, including the following:

+.50 between verbal identification of patterns and serial memory of pictures.

+.82 between spelling and verbal recognition of letters.

+.69 between serial memory of pictures and the ability to write letters.

+.56 between ability to write letters and spelling.

+.57 between spelling and serial memory of pictures.

+.69 between serial memory of gestures and serial memory of pictures.

Data of this nature indicate that there are common elements in many of the tasks, including visual memory independent of the stimulus to be remembered, and serial memory ability independent of specific stimuli to be correctly ordered.

Revised Battery of Tests

As a result of the preliminary tests and analysis of the data obtained, a final battery of tests was constructed which excluded the tests of persistence used in the initial testing and substituted a test of line walking, i.e. "How slowly can you walk this line?" The child was clocked to the nearest tenth of a second.

Administration procedures of the other tests were made more exact and refined. The tests of serial memory ability were changed in the following manner: The child was started with three stimuli (either gestures or pictures), and the final presentation consisted of seven instead of six stimuli (i.e., gestures or pictures), as it was found that none of the children failed to name or imitate two stimuli in correct order and, at the same time, a number of the children in the preliminary testing could correctly order six stimuli.

The twenty-nine children selected for the study were tested and retested (the following day) in January on this revised battery.

A preliminary survey of the data revealed that the most difficult letters to identify orally were "Q" (missed by nine children), "U" and "V" (missed by seven), "J" (missed by six) and "D," "H," "L," "P" and "Z" (missed by five children). The most difficult letter of the lower case to write after it was visually presented was "q" (four children missed it).

The most difficult patterns to verbally identify included the half-circle, rectangle and diamond (each was missed by fifteen children) and the square (missed by eight). Only two children failed to identify a triangle, and only one could not name a circle when it was shown.

Tallies of the serial memory tasks revealed, as would be expected, the fact that the most difficult stimuli to reproduce were those within the middle parts of the series.

A summary of the mean scores and the correlations between the first and second testing sessions is seen in Table XXXV. As can be seen, most of the tests reached acceptable levels of reliability, with the exception of serial memory of gestures and verbal identification of patterns. Learning affects are seen when contrasting the scores of serial memory for pictures and the persistence scores obtained in the first and second testing periods, although these shifts are not statistically significant because of the standard deviations obtained.

A correlation matrix was computed using the Pearson Product Moment Formula and is presented in Table XXXVI. As can be seen and might be expected, significant positive correlations were achieved when scores obtained from verbal recognition of letters were contrasted with serial memory for pictures ($r = .71$) and when spelling scores were compared to those obtained from the test of verbal identification of letters ($r = .61$). The ability

TABLE XXXV

COMPARISON OF TEST-RETEST SCORES USING TWENTY-NINE
CHILDREN DURING THE INITIAL TEST PERIOD,
JANUARY 1969

	1st Testing M.	S.D.	2nd Testing M.	S.D.	r
1. Body perception	7.79	1.93	7.96	2.17	0.80
2. Gross agility	8.00	2.43	7.31	2.32	0.82
3. Balance	7.27	1.62	7.24	2.00	0.80
4. Locomotor agility	9.06	1.05	9.03	1.06	0.82
5. Persistence, line walking for time	26.00	9.00	30.96	15.46	0.80
6. Visual recognition of patterns	5.68	0.91	5.79	0.82	0.87
7. Verbal identification of patterns	2.82	1.16	3.00	1.11	0.71
8. Verbal identification of letters	22.72	5.45	22.86	5.49	0.99
9. Written replication of letters	24.72	1.72	25.03	1.61	0.88
10. Serial memory of pictures	20.51	6.23	22.06	5.47	0.81
11. Serial memory of gestures	22.86	3.22	22.93	3.20	0.69
12. Spelling (N=19) 20 words	10.00	5.07	9.36	4.55	0.95

to write letters and serial memory for pictures was also highly correlated ($r = .82$), as were the two tasks of serial memory (pictures and gestures $r = .56$).

An interesting negative correlation was obtained when the scores from the "attention" test were compared to the spelling test ($r = .57$). This may have been indicative of the fact that many of the children are habitually underaroused for efficient learning, i.e., the slowest line-walkers tended to be the poorest spellers.

Other positive and significant (at the 5% level) correlations were obtained when scores from the locomotor agility test were compared to scores obtained from the body-perception test ($r = .59$), where gross agility was contrasted to locomotor agility ($r = .37$), and when locomotor agility was compared to the ability to write letters of the alphabet ($r = .53$). The last correlation may indicate some common element involving visual-motor coordination common to both jumping for accuracy into squares (leg-eye) and drawing letters (hand-eye).

TABLE XXXVI

CORRELATION COEFFICIENTS BETWEEN SUBTESTS USED IN FINAL TEST BATTERY (N=29)

	Gross Agility	Balance	Locomot. Agil.	Persist. Line Walking	Vis. Recog. Patt.	Verb. Identi. Patt.	Verb. Identi. Lett.	Writt. Replic. Lett.	Ser. Memory Pict.	Ser. Memory Gest.	Spell.
Body perception	21.	.23	.59	.03	-.04	.27	.16	.34	.31	.03	.27
Gross agility		.18	.37	.14	.04	.05	.30	.28	.40	.32	-.17
Balance			.16	.14	.00	.27	-.01	.30	.16	.02	-.15
Locomotor agility				.12	.31	.27	.17	.53	.40	.35	-.05
Persistence, line walking for time					.23	.08	-.05	.36	.32	.30	-.59
Visual recognition of patterns						.00	.01	.24	.21	.28	-.29
Verbal identification of patterns							.09	.17	.10	-.01	.07
Written replication of letters								.42	.71	.37	.61
Serial memory of pictures									.82	.36	.02
Serial memory of gestures										.56	.06
Spelling (N=19)											-.08

Facilities and Equipment

The following patterns were painted on the floor of the cafeteria: a spelling grid containing upper case letters, a second grid containing lower case letters, and geometric figures constructed of yellow lining tape, as shown. In addition, three mats (4' x 6') were used which contained grid markings as drawn. Three rubber playground balls were also used, as were hoops and the like.

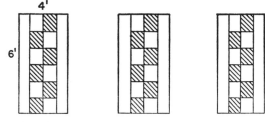

The space utilized measured thirty feet by thirty feet and the grids, mats and geometric figures were placed as shown.

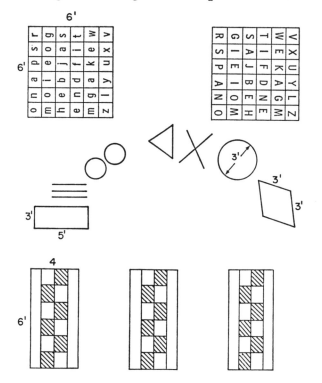

PROGRAM PROCEDURES

Following preliminary testing as described in the previous pages, the children were separated into groups composed of five to six children each. Each group was taken from a larger class of forty students. From February 2nd to March 17th the group classes met Monday, Wednesday and Friday for one-half hour each session. A total of five classes were conducted each of these days. The younger children in grades one and two were initially given tasks intended to reduce hyperactivity, to aid them in identifying body parts and the left-right dimensions of their body and in training in the alphabet, serial memory tasks and practice in pattern recognition. A typical lesson plan, lasting thirty minutes for this group, is as follows:

Eight minutes—*Impulse Control Activities*: "How slowly can you move?" "Tighten and relax your muscles." "How loose can you make your muscles?"

Eight minutes—*Pattern Recognition*: "Can you run and stand in the triangle?" "Can you skip to the square?" "Can you walk around the triangle and count its sides?"

Five minutes—*Serial Memory Practice*: "Can you do the same things with a ball in each of the patterns as Jean did?"

Nine minutes—*Alphabet Training*: "Can you jump in the proper squares while saying the alphabet?" "Edward, watch Monica and tell me whether she is going to the letter I call out."

The older groups during this initial period concentrated upon tasks involving serial memory, impulse control, letter identification and spelling. A typical lesson plan for this group was as follows:

Six minutes—*Impulse Control Activities and Relaxation Training.*

Eight minutes—*Serial Memory Practice.*

Eight minutes—*Letter Recognition,* using grids.

Eight minutes—*Spelling Practice*: "Jump and spell the words I give you."

The content of the program was derived from several publications by Cratty and Martin and by Cratty (11, 7, 8, 10). The monograph *Movement, Perception and Thought* aided in perceiving the sequencing of various activities and in the rationale for the manner in which transfer of one cognitive skill to another might be achieved (8). A package of fifty game cards provided specific games and subskills which might be utilized in the numbered grid (9). Chapter 5, "The Adjustment of Arousal Level and the Improvement of Attention," in *Perceptual-Motor Efficiency in Children,* by Cratty and Martin provided a rationale and activities to be used when aiding the children to gain better self-control and to reduce hyperactivity (11).

Identification of Children Needing Special Attention

By the end of the second week it was becoming apparent to the teacher/experimenter that eight of the children needed special attention if they were to master the academic operations which confronted them. Thus these eight children were, in addition to the three-day-a-week class, given special help individually on Tuesday and Thursday for thirty minutes with the teacher-experimenter.

Mid-program Screening Test

Five weeks following the organizational change outlined above, all twenty-nine children were given pass-fail screening tests to determine the extent of the progress (if any) that was being made. These tests consisted of verbal memory of the alphabet, pattern recognition and left-right discrimination.

Final Organization of Instructional Program

For the remainder of the semester, March 28th until May 31st, all twenty-nine children remained in the groups taught Monday, Wednesday and Friday mornings and, in addition, the eight childern who had been given special help were also afforded this one-to-one teacher-pupil ratio until the end of the semester (in addition to participating in the three-day-a-week group classes).

RESULTS

The findings are divided into three sections. First, group changes from pre- to posttest are described. Secondly, an examination of the children who initially scored lowest in several of the tests will be surveyed relative to the change evidenced in their posttest scores. The third section of the results contains several case studies in which children who scored lowest in several of the test categories are described and the changes evidenced in their posttests are discussed. Throughout the following section the reader must keep in mind that no adequate control groups were used and that the change described could be due to a number of factors independent of the teaching variables imposed.*

Group Changes

As can be seen in Table XXXVII, changes significant at or exceeding the 5 percent level of confidence were recorded on nine out of thirteen tests administered when the total group of children's scores were contrasted. Only in the tests of serial memory ability of gestures, in the visual recognition of various geometric patterns, in the locomotor agility subtest of the motor battery and in spelling words were significant changes not recorded. However, even when the pre- and posttest scores of these four tests were compared, the changes occurred in the expected direction.

The most marked changes were recorded in the children's ability to verbally identify various geometric figures, in their verbal identification of body parts, in their overall motor ability scores, in their serial memory ability for pictures and in their written and verbal responses to the visual presentations of letters of the alphabet.

The data indicates that as a group the children learned to move more slowly when walking the line in the purported measures of impulse control. As a group, too, they learned to better recognize letters of the alphabet when visually presented,

---

* Instructor personality, learning how to take the tests, special attention accorded the subjects, etc. These variables will be discussed more thoroughly in the section which follows the results.

TABLE XXXVII

COMPARISON OF PRE- AND POSTTEST SCORES OF THE
TOTAL SUBJECTS (N=29)

		Pretest		Posttest		t
		M.	*S.D.*	*M.*	*S.D.*	
1.	Body perception	7.71	1.91	8.96	1.21	3.47*
2.	Cratty Battery					
	a. Gross agility	7.93	2.45	8.96	0.98	2.35*
	b. Balance	7.18	1.54	7.97	1.38	2.59*
	c. Locomotor agility	9.06	0.99	8.64	1.40	1.85
	d. Gross motor total	24.14	3.13	25.61	2.26	2.72*
3.	Impulse control	25.79	9.21	38.06	24.84	3.08*
4.	Pattern recognition					
	a. Verbal	2.79	1.15	5.50	0.82	12.40*
	b. Visual	5.68	0.85	5.96	0.19	1.74
5.	Letter recognition					
	a. Verbal	22.61	5.50	25.00	3.06	2.97*
	b. Written	24.68	1.68	25.64	0.75	3.35*
6.	Serial memory ability					
	a. Picture	20.36	6.26	22.57	4.95	2.52
	b. Gesture	22.68	3.32	23.79	2.36	1.98
7.	Spelling (N=19)	10.00	3.22	11.28	4.56	2.04

* Differences significant at 5 percent level.

and could write them and verbally repeat them more accurately following the educational regime imposed.

Pre- and Posttest Differences, by Sex

Tables XXXVIII and XXXIX present the findings, with the data separated by sex. Due to the small number of subjects in each group many of the differences are not statistically significant, and yet only one of the thirteen test scores (locomotor agility) obtained from both the boys and the girls failed to evidence change in the expected direction. Application of the nonparametric sign test, which evaluates significance in data on a plus-minus basis, clearly delineates the fact that improvement (a plus score) on twelve out of the thirteen tests is significant statistically (at the 5% level).

Analyzed by test, Table XXXVIII indicates that statistically significant changes were recorded in pre- and posttest scores by the boys in measures evaluating the perception (verbal identification) of body parts, impulse control, the verbal identification of geometric figures and both verbal and written responses to letters (both letter recognition tests). Additionally, the boys' spelling scores improved significantly from an average of 7.4 out of 20 correct, to 9.1 correct, without specific practice on the words in the list used in the test.

The girls, on the other hand, evidenced significant improvement in tests evaluating body perception, impulse control, the verbal identification of the geometric figures and the ability to remember a series of pictures in the proper order.

When both the pre- and posttest scores were compared by sex, it was found that only in the measure of spelling competency were significant differences discovered. In both the pre- and posttests the girls were significantly better than the boys, as can be seen when comparing Table XXXVIII and Tables XXXIX (t = 4.0 and 4.1 respectively). In all the other scores obtained there were no significant sex differences when both the pre- and posttest measures were compared.

TABLE XXXVIII

COMPARISON OF PRE- AND POSTTEST SCORES OF THE BOYS (N=17)

		Pretest		Posttest		r	t
		M.	S.D.	M.	S.D.		
1.	Body perception	7.47	1.98	8.68	1.33	0.31	2.34*
2.	Cratty Battery						
	a. Gross agility	8.47	1.95	9.12	0.91	0.41	1.45
	b. Balance	7.29	1.49	7.82	1.30	0.55	1.59
	c. Locomotor agility	8.71	1.02	8.41	1.50	0.70	1.09
	d. Gross motor total	24.47	2.96	25.41	2.51	0.72	1.81
3.	Impulse control	27.00	10.35	39.57	27.52	0.60	2.20*
4.	Pattern recognition						
	a. Verbal	2.59	1.24	5.29	0.89	0.32	8.46*
	b. Visual	5.76	0.55	6.00	0		1.72
5.	Letter recognition						
	a. Verbal	21.29	6.42	24.35	3.79	0.66	2.52
	b. Written	24.53	1.43	25.53	0.79	0.14	2.61
6.	Serial memory ability						
	a. Picture	19.82	6.92	21.65	5.83	0.67	1.39
	b. Gesture	22.94	2.92	23.47	2.73	0.54	0.78
7.	Spelling (N=12)	7.42	3.89	9.17	3.89	0.77	2.18*

* Differences significant at 5 percent level.

Analysis of Improvement of the Less Able Subjects

Although inspection of the data indicative of group changes presented on the previous pages might be considered highly encouraging, it also might be hypothesized that the improvement seen was evidenced only by children within the subject population who were close to the average score or above average in

TABLE XXXIX

COMPARISON OF PRE- AND POSTTEST SCORES OF THE GIRLS (N=11)

		Pretest		Posttest		r	t
		M.	S.D.	M.	S.D.		
1.	Body perception	8.09	1.73	9.45	0.79	0.38	2.68*
2.	Cratty Battery						
	a. Gross agility	7.00	2.88	8.73	1.05	0.25	1.85
	b. Balance	7.00	1.60	8.18	1.47	0.31	2.07
	c. Locomotor agility	9.56	0.66	9.00	1.13	0.37	1.59
	d. Gross motor total	23.64	3.13	25.91	1.78	0.17	2.06
3.	Impulse control	23.91	6.67	35.73	19.76	0.57	2.22*
4.	Pattern recognition						
	a. Verbal	3.09	0.90	5.82	0.577	0.39	10.03*
	b. Visual	5.55	1.16	5.91	0.29	0.16	1.01
5.	Letter recognition						
	a. Verbal	24.64	2.54	26.00	0		1.71
	b. Written	24.91	1.98	25.82	0.58	0.94	1.98
6.	Serial memory ability						
	a. Picture	21.18	4.97	24.00	2.56	0.85	2.87
	b. Gesture	22.27	3.82	24.27	1.49	0.71	2.14
7.	Spelling (N=6)	12.17	3.39	15.50	2.22	0.81	0.36

* Differences significant at 5 percent level.

each of the tests administered. In other terms it might be assumed that the children of average and above-average ability (within this below-average population) showed improvement, while the extremely deficient child did not or could not under the conditions outlined.

In an effort to determine whether these less able subjects evidenced improvement the following analyses were made of children scoring within the lower one-third of the scores for the various tests, and, in addition, individual analyses are made of the pre- and posttest scores of the one or two children who evidenced the poorest scores in the various tests given. Due to the small number of subjects within these less able populations no formal statistical analyses were carried out, and the discussion is based only upon inspection of mean score changes.

Body Perception

Twelve children scored at 7 or below on the 10-point-possible body perception test. Thus these children evidenced an inability to correctly identify their left and right sides, arms and legs. Additionally, they could not cross their body and, for example, touch their left hand to the right knee.

These children were distributed between the various grades

as follows: five were first graders, three were second graders, three were third graders and one was a fourth grader. Only one of the children was a Mexican-American (a third-grade boy), while the remainder were Negro children. Seven of the group were boys.

The average body-perception scores of these children in their pretest was 6.08, while the posttest mean was 9.08 (S.D.s respectively were 1.7 and 2.2). Thus it appears that the group as a whole improved to a marked degree, and when the program was completed could achieve almost a perfect score on a test of body perception which included making complex left-right judgments about their body parts.

The lowest scorer in this test was a first-grade boy who scored 1 (out of a possible 10 points) the first time he was exposed to the test. His final score, following the educational program, was 8.

Motor Ability Traits

Three tests of motor ability were administered; one a test of balance and two agility tests. One of the agility tests evaluated the ability to hop and jump with accuracy (locomotor agility) and the second purportedly reflected what was termed "gross agility," which was composed of two subtests evaluating a child's ability to move up and down rapidly and accurately (i.e. "How fast can you get up?") from a back-lying positioning.

Gross Agility

Eight children—three first grades, one second grader, one third grader and two fourth graders—scored 7 or less out of 10 possible points on this test. Five were girls and two were boys. (In previous studies it was found that boys did better on this measure, as one of the subtests involves leg power and abdominal strength usually found to be better in even younger boys.) All of these low-scoring children were Negroes.

The pretest mean for this group was 4.5, while the final mean was 8.6 (exceeding the norm for children of this age group). The distribution measures (S.D.) were 1.7 and 1.1 for the pre- and posttests respectively. The two lowest scorers in this test, a first-grade girl and a fourth-grade girl, achieved a score of 2 in the pretest, while their final scores were 7 and 9 respectively. Again these two lowest achievers also had final scores which equalled the norms for children of their age and sex.

BALANCE

Twelve children scored a 6 or below on the balance test (10 points possible). A score of 6 generally indicated inability to engage in a one-foot stand with eyes closed for any length of time, a task usually not possible for children under the age of seven. Thus, as would be expected, one-half of these twelve low-scorers were in the first grade, two in the second grade, three in the third grade and one in the fourth. Also, as would be expected, seven of these twelve children were boys. Two of these twelve children were Mexican-American, a second-grade boy and a third-grade boy, with the remainder Negro.

The pretest mean score of this low-ability group was 5.7 (S.D. .61) and the final mean score they posted was 7.5 (S.D. 1.40). The lowest scores in this group posting initial scores of 5 were a first-grade boy, a second-grade boy and a fourth-grade girl, and they all had final scores of 7 on this test.

LOCOMOTOR AGILITY

Nine children scored 8 and 7 on the locomotor agility test (top score of 10 points). These consisted of three first graders, four second graders, one third graders and one fourth grader. Eight out of these nine children were boys, as would be expected.* Two of the nine children were Mexican-American and the remaining seven were Negro.

The initial mean of this low-ability group was 7.7, while the posttest mean was 7.4 (S.D.s were .43 and 1.34, respectively). These data thus indicate that no significant improvement in this attribute was evidenced; however, it should be remembered that, in general, the initial scores of these so-called low-ability groups were superior to norms collected from Caucasian children, and thus little improvement was expected.

----

* Generally, most studies have shown that boys are inferior to girls in tasks of this nature, indicating either superior neurological maturity or reflecting the inclination of girls to participate more and for more extended periods of time in activities such as hopscotch and the like than boys.

The two children scoring 7 initially on this test were both first-grade boys, and their second scores were 6 and 8.

Total Motor Ability Score

A total motor ability score was computed by combining the three scores discussed above, so that the maximum possible score was 30. Eight children scored 23 or less points on this combined test. Four of these were first graders (two boys and two girls), two second graders (boys) and two fourth graders (girls). All of these low-scoring children were Negroes.

The initial mean score of this low-scoring group was 20.22 (S.D. 1.98), the final mean score posted was 24.44 (S.D. 2.4). The lowest-scoring children were a first-grade boy with a score of 16 (out of 30 possible), a first-grade girl with a score of 18 and a fourth-grade girl with a score of 19, and three posted final scores of 25, 27 and 19 respectively.

Impulse Control

The test of impulse control was obtained by asking the children to walk a line twelve feet long "as slowly as you can." It was assumed that the children exhibiting less well-developed self-control would walk it fastest, while the children exhibiting "good" impulse control could, or would, walk more slowly.

The range of the scores obtained was 14 seconds to 52 seconds. The poorest scores were evidenced by eight children who walked the line in 19 seconds or faster. Four of these were first graders (three boys and a girl), one a third grader (girl) and three fourth graders (two girls and a boy.) All of these children were Negroes.

The initial mean of this "fast-moving" group was 17.25 seconds (S.D. 2.04), while the final mean was 20.70 seconds (S.D. 8.9). It should be noted that the distribution measure changed significantly the second time the test was administered, thus the effects of the training appeared to have highly individual effects upon these children.

The fastest children included a fourth-grade boy moving along the line initially in 14 seconds and two first-grade children (a boy and a girl) who walked the twelve feet in 15 seconds. They posted final scores of 7.2, 18.5 and 18.0 seconds respectively, which further emphasized the highly individual nature of the change elicited in various children.

Pattern Recognition, Visual Comparison

Most of the children could visually recognize and correctly compare six geometric patterns. Twenty-four could do this perfectly, while only three missed one of the patterns. The task consisted of observing various patterns presented one at a time by the experimenter and then pointing to the corresponding pattern on a sheet placed in front of them.

Two children, however, seemed to have difficulty in this task during this first test period (a fourth-grade boy and a fourth-grade girl). One could only visually identify two out of the six correctly, while the second compared four out of six correctly. On the final testing both of the children achieved perfect scores on this test of pattern recognition.

Verbal Identification of Six Geometric Patterns

More difficult for the twenty-nine children was the correct naming of the six common geometric forms presented to them one at a time. Eleven out of the twenty-nine, for example, scored 2 (out of 6) or below on this test, while one child, a fourth-grade boy, could not name any forms correctly in the initial test of this attribute. Three of these eleven low-scoring children were first graders, two boys and a girl; three were second-grade boys; three were third graders, two boys and a girl; and two were fourth grade children (a boy and a girl.) All three Mexican-American children in the twenty-nine-child sample were in the low-scoring group in this test. The remaining eight were Negro.

The initial mean score of this low-ability group was 1.63 (S.D. .64), while the final mean of these eleven children was 5.18 (S.D. .94). Thus, by the final testing, the children as a group could verbally identify 5 out of the 6 geometric figures correctly, while their initial testing revealed that, on the average, they could only identify 2 out of 6 correctly. The lowest-scoring children were a third-grade boy who could not identify any of the figures verbally and a second-grade boy and a third-grade boy who could only name one. The final score of all three children was 5 out of 6 geometric figures correctly named.

Letter Recognition

Two tests of letter recognition were given. In one the child was asked to verbally identify uppercase letters presented one at a time and then removed from view while the child attempted to name them. The second was a test of the child's ability to write lower case letters presented in the same way and then removed while the child attempted to write them one at a time.

VERBAL RESPONSE TO UPPERCASE LETTERS

Eleven of the children failed to correctly name four or more of the letters. Five of these children were in the first grade (three boys and two girls), two in the second grade (boys), two were in the third grade (boys) and one was in the fourth grade (boy). None of these eleven children was Mexican-American and eight out of the eleven were boys.

The pretest mean of this low-ability group was 16.9 letters correctly named, while the posttest mean was 23.3 correctly named letters.

Three of these eleven children scored extremely low in this test. Two first graders (a boy and a girl) could only name 6 and 7 letters respectively when they were shown them, while a second-grade boy could only name 14 correctly. Two of the three final scores of these children were highly encouraging The child who initially could only name 7 letters correctly named all 26 letters the second time tested. The child who named only 14 correct initially got a final score of 22. However, the first-grade boy who initially named only 6 letters in the first testing posted a score of only 10 after the training period to which he had been exposed.

WRITTEN RESPONSE TO LOWERCASE LETTERS

In general the twenty-nine children posted better scores on this test of letter recognition, as their task was only to copy a lowercase letter after it was presented visually to them. It is thus uncertain whether the scores obtained reflected ability to copy geometric figures, or whether there was a real identification of the letters presented. In any case, eighteen of the twenty-eight children copied 25 out of 26 letters correctly, thus the low-ability group in this test consisted of children who scored 24 or below.

Four of these ten children were in the first grade (three boys and a girl), two were in second grade (boys) and three were in third grade (two boys and a girl). None of the low-ability group was in the fourth grade and one was a Mexican-American.

The initial score of this low-ability group was 22.66 (S.D. of 1.50); the final score of the group was 25.22 (S.D. .92). One of the children, a first-grade girl, could only copy 19 out of the 26 lowercase letters correctly during the initial test period. Her final score was 24.

Serial Memory Ability

Two tests of serial memory ability were given, one in which the child was asked to duplicate a series of gestures and the second in which they had to name in proper order a series of animal pictures. A perfect score in each of these tests was 26.

MEMORY FOR PICTURES

Ten of the twenty-eight children posted scores of 21 and below in this test. Six of these were first graders (three boys and three girls), one was a second-grade girl, one a third-grade girl, one a third-grade boy and the tenth was a fourth-grade girl. One of the ten was a Mexican-American child (the third-grade boy) and the remainder were Negro children.

The initial mean score for these ten children was 14.10 (S.D. 6.8) and the final mean score for the ten children was 19.60 (S.D. 7.21). Four of the children posted extremely low scores. A first-grade girl could remember only 1 (out of a possible 26), a third-grade boy scored 4, another first-grade girl had an initial score of 8 and a first-grade boy had a score of 9 the first time they were tested.

The second time these four children were tested the child scoring 1 did not improve, the child scoring 4 initially had a final score of 20, the child with a first score of 8 had a second score of 16, while the child initially scoring 9 had a final score of 22.

MEMORY FOR GESTURES

As a group the twenty-eight children remembered gestures better than they did a series of pictures. None of the children, for example, scored below 13 on this test (out of 26 possible) and one-half (14) had a score of 25. The "low-ability" group posted scores of 21 or less on this test and was composed of eight children. Four of the eight were first graders (two boys and two girls), one was a second-grade boy, one a third-grade girl and two were fourth graders (one boy and one girl).

The initial mean score of this group was 18.00 (S.D. 2.54) and the final mean score was 22.25 (S.D. 3.56). The child scoring only thirteen initially on this test (a fourth-grade girl) had a score of 20 the final time she was tested.

Spelling

The ten first-grade children were not scored initially in spelling, as it would not be expected that they could spell any of the words on the list during their first semester at school. The low-ability group analyzed thus consisted of six children who only spelled from 2 to 5 words correctly out of the 20 which were presented to them. Two were second graders (both girls), three were third graders, of whom one was a boy, and two were fourth graders (a boy and a girl). One of the children was a Mexican-American, the fourth-grade boy. The initial mean score of this group was 3.66 (S.D. .94), while the final mean was 6.5 (S.D. 3.6). The size of the second standard reveals that the improvement in this attribute among these children was a highly individual matter. Analysis of individual scores among this group of six reveals the following:

Pretest Score	Posttest Score
2	5
3	3
4	11
4	5
5	12

It thus appears that only four of the six childern improved to a marked degree in spelling ability. The implications of this finding will be discussed in the section which follows.

Summary of the Results

1. Group changes significant at the 5 percent level of confidence were recorded in the expected direction on nine out of the thirteen tests administered.

2. Significant improvement was recorded in scores reflecting body perception, three motor ability scores, a measure of impulse control, verbal identification of letters, the ability to copy lowercase letters, the ability to name common geometric figures and the ability to remember a series of pictures presented one at a time.

3. Significant improvement was evidenced by the boys in measures of body perception, impulse control, verbal identification of geometric figures and in both verbal and written responses to uppercase and lowercase letters presented one at a time. The boy's spelling scores improved significantly.

4. Significant improvement was evidenced by the girls in measures of body perception, impulse control, verbal identification of geometric figures and the serial memory of pictures.

5. Analysis of the scores of the less able children taking the various tests revealed that they evidenced marked improvement in the tests given, with the exception of spelling.

SUMMARY, CONCLUSIONS, AND IMPLICATIONS

Twenty-nine children with an average I.Q. of 75 were exposed to a program of total body movement purporting to enhance selected academic skills. The three-lesson-a-week program, lasting seventeen weeks, was preceded and followed by a program containing thirteen tests of academic and motor attributes.

The educational program consisted of activities purporting to enhance impulse control, body perception, serial memory abilities, letter and pattern recognition and spelling. The activities were those in which total body movement was involved and, for example, consisted of walking around triangles and counting the sides, remembering and performing a series of movement performed by another child, and jumping in grids containing letters of the alphabet.

Analysis of the group data indicated that significant positive changes in nine out of the thirteen tests had occurred. Further detailed inspection of the data elicited from children who scored low on each of the tests indicated that marked improvement had been evidenced in all of the tests, with the exception of spelling.

Although it might be concluded that the program of gross motor activity had a highly positive effect upon the attributes measured, it is believed not sound to form this type of conclusion in the absence of proper controls. The data do, however, offer highly interesting avenues for further investigation in which such variables as instructor rapport, visual inspection of the training facilities and the motivating effect of playing games are controlled for.

Many implications for further research and for improved teaching methodology arose from the data and from observations of the children and of the general teaching environment. For example, it was noted that teaching the names of the various geometric patterns may be a superfluous academic exercise which leads nowhere. Unless transfer is specifically taught for, i.e. how a triangle may be modified to make the letter "A," the geometric patterns simply constitute additional "letters" for the children to learn and thus have little educational significance.

The lack of improvement in the spelling scores can be explained by the fact that spelling was only engaged in (by jumping into the letters on the grid) during the final week of the program. At the same time the data suggest that particularly with the younger and less able children, spelling of specific words must be concentrated upon or little general learning of how to spell is likely to occur.

Further studies should also illuminate whether practice in serial memory ability involving movements (of the body, or of limb gestures) is likely to transfer to other more academic serial memory tasks (i.e. remembering the order of letters in words). The present data suggest that serial memory ability is likely to be highly specific to the stimuli involved and to the manner in which the subject must replicate the series of stimuli.

It was also felt that the initial two weeks of the program were needed before the highly active children could be placed under some type of control and before any learning or learning games could be engaged in. Thus various exercises in impulse control and relaxation training were engaged in during these first weeks. Only after this instructor control was accepted by the children could additional exercises in impulse control and in learning games take place. It was thus believed that the general shape of the learning curve which was elicited (and which will be confirmed in future studies) was a positively accelerated one. The improvement in the various attributes trained for was greatest during the final weeks of the educational program administered.

A number of methodological implications arose from the instructor's observations. For example, it was obvious that the children were able to identify letters largely by their fixed location on the painted grids. In the future, it is planned to have movable letters placed on squares which can be transferred to various locations within the grid so that place cues are subordinate to the cues arising from the configurations of the letters themselves.

Within this same context, it is planned in future studies to require the children in the middle and upper elementary years to identify cursive letters in addition to lowercase and uppercase letters used in this study.

The lack of improvement in the ability to write letters on the part of many children indicated that the teaching techniques employed should be combined with various desk-top writing tasks for maximum transfer to various classroom operations required of the child. For example, after jumping in the proper squares, the child might then be asked to sit down and write the letters he has just "visited" via his locomotor efforts.

BIBLIOGRAPHY

1. ————: Doman-Delacato treatment of neurologically handicapped children. American Academy of Pediatrics Executive Board Statement. *AAP News Letter, 16*:11, 1965.

2. ————: The Doman-Delacato treatment of neurologically handicapped children. *Arch Phys Med, 49*:183-186, 1968.

3. ANDERSON, RUSSEL W.: *Effects of Neuro-Psychological Techniques on Reading Achievement.* Greeley, Colo., Colorado State College, doctoral dissertation, 1965.

4. BARSCH, RAY H.: *Achieving Perceptual-Motor Efficiency, A Space-Oriented Approach to Learning.* Seattle, Special Child, 1967.

5. BROWN, ROSCOE: The effect of a perceptual-motor education program on perceptual-motor skills and reading readiness. Paper presented to Research Section, AAHPER, St. Louis, Missouri, April 1, 1968.

6. CORDER, W. D.: Effects of physical education on the intellectual, physical and social development of educable mentally retarded boys. Unpublished special project, George Peabody College, Nashville, Tennessee, 1965.

7. CRATTY, BRYANT J.: *Motor Activity and the Education of Retardates.* Philadelphia, Lea & F., 1969.

8. CRATTY, BRYANT J.: *Movement, Perception and Thought.* Palo Alto, Peek Publications, 1969.

9. CRATTY, BRYANT J.: *Moving and Learning, Fifty Games for Children with Learning Difficulties.* Freeport, Long Island, Educational Activities, 1968.

10. CRATTY, BRYANT J.: *Perceptual-Motor Behavior and Educational Processes,* Springfield, Thomas, 1969.

11. CRATTY, BRYANT J., AND MARTIN, SISTER MARGARET M.: *Perceptual-Motor Efficiency in Children.* Philadelphia, Lea & F., 1969.

12. DELACATO, CARL H.: *The Diagnosis and Treatment of Speech and Reading Problems.* Springfield, Thomas, 1963.

13. GETMAN, G. N.: *How to Develop Your Child's Intelligence.* Luverne, Minnesota, G. N. Getman, 1962.

14. HUMPHREY, JAMES H.: Comparison of the use of active games and language workbook exercises as learning media in the development of language understanding with third grade children. *Percept Motor Skills, 21*:23-26, 1965.

15. KEPHART, NEWELL C.: *The Slow Learner in the Classroom.* Columbus, Ohio, Merrill, C. E., 1960.

16. KERSHNER, JOHN R.: Doman-Delacato's theory of neurological organization applied with retarded children. *Exceptional Child, 33*:441-450, 1968.

17. MONTESSORI, MARIA: *Dr. Montessori's Own Handbook.* New York, Frederick A. Stokes, 1914.

18. OLIVER, JAMES N.: The effects of physical conditioning exercises and activities on the mental characteristics of educationally sub-normal boys. *Brit J Educ Psychol, 29*:15-165, 1958.

19. RARICK, G. LAWRENCE, AND BROADHEAD, GEOFFREY D.: *The Effects of Individualized Versus Group Oriented Physical Education Programs on Selected Parameters of the Development of Educable Mentally Retarded and Minimally Brain Injured Children.* Sponsored by the United States Office of Education and Joseph P. Kennedy Jr. Foundation, 1968.

20. ROACH, EUGENE G.: Evaluation of an experimental program of perceptual-motor training with slow readers. In Figurel, J. Allen

(Ed.): *Vistas in Reading.* International Reading Association Conference Proceedings, XI, 1966, 446-450.
21. ROBBINS, M. P., AND GLASS, G. V.: The Doman-Delacato rationale: a critical analysis. In Hellmuth, Jerome (Ed.): *Educational Therapy,* vol. 2. Seattle, Special Child, 1968.
22. ROBERTS, R. W., AND COLEMAN, J. C.: Investigation of the role of visual and kinesthetic factors in reading failure. *J Educ Res, 51*:445-451, 1958.
23. RUTHERFORD, WM. D.: Perceptual-motor training and readiness. In Figurel, J. Allen (Ed.): *Reading and Inquiry.* International Reading Association Conference Proceedings, X, 1965, 194-196.
24. SOLOMON, A., AND PRANGLE, R.: Demonstrations of physical fitness improvement in the EMR. *Exceptional Child, 33*:177-181, 1967.
25. YARBOROUGH, BETTY H.: A study of the effectiveness of the Leavell Language-Development Service in improving the silent reading ability and other language skills of persons with mixed dominance. Doctoral dissertation, Ed.D., University of Virginia, Charlottesville, 1964.

PART TWO
SELECTED ESSAYS

Chapter V

COGNITION AND MOTOR LEARNING*

A NUMBER OF theoretical positions relating thought and movement may be found in the philosophical, historical and experimental literature. The philosophers of ancient Greece evidenced a mind-body monism which was reflected in their statues of the human figure on which shrewd faces were placed above well-muscled torsos.

The Christian Idealist of the pre-Renaissance period espoused a separatism of mind, body and spirit. Educators today who embrace this same philosophy are usually found to be inserting physical activity into their programs only to be dispelling the muscular energies that prove "harmful" to the most important job of the school, the development of the mind.

In the eighteenth and nineteenth centuries the pendulum swung in the other direction. Pestalozzi, Rousseau and others developed educational programs which were based upon the supposition that a child's mind and body interacted as a unity. The organismic and biosocial theories outlined in more recent times by Olson and Gardner Murphy are contemporary statements of this monistic approach (34, 32).

Movement and cognition may be discussed in more pragmatic terms. Some have attempted to discover just how the intellectual processes contribute in the development of physical skills, while, conversely, others have attempted to ascertain just how motor activities may contribute to the development of the intellect (6, 16, 29).

Experimenters and theoreticians dealing with these two diverse but related questions have sometimes been guilty of

---

* Speech presented to the Second International Symposium on Biomechanics at Eindhoven, Holland, August 25, 1969, by B. J. Cratty.

oversimplification and/or misinterpretation of their findings. For example, in the literature on the subject some have suggested that movement is the basis of the intellect when low non-predictive correlations are obtained between complex movement tasks (requiring the chaining together of a number of responses) and scores obtained from intelligence tests (containing tasks whose successful execution also depends upon serial memory ability) (18, 19).

Others have claimed to have raised the I.Q.s of retardates by exposing them to movement experiences, when in truth the personality of the experimenter and the extra attention he afforded the subjects were probably more influential of change than was the program of motor activities.

One of the central issues when examining mind-body relationships is the delineation of the importance of movement in the development of the total human personality from birth to maturity. While it is self-evident that infants and young children explore their world in direct ways through movement, there is impressive evidence that motor activity and motor learning represent a component of, rather than the central support of, the human personality. Thus we advance two hypotheses for your consideration: (1) Movement will aid a child to think to the extent to which thought accompanies his movements; (2) Thought will aid skill to the extent to which cognition is encouraged at opportune times within the learning process.

Worthy of examination are some of the investigations whose findings suggest that skill learning occurs within the central rather than within the peripheral portions of the nervous system.* It should also be productive to review some of the recent investigations whose data point to helpful ways in which thought may be inserted into motor learning practice (10).

Several investigations carried out with animals have produced data which suggest that learning may occur through silent observation as well as through the direct and active participation

---

* There is a considerable amount of neurological evidence supporting the fact that voluntary movements are always mediated by the higher brain centers, despite how much skill is achieved.

of the learner. An interesting series of studies employed cats who learned to emerge from escape boxes by pushing against sticks that released levers. Cats in a second group were placed in cages adjacent to the cages of the cats in the first group and were permitted to observe the attempts of the first group to escape. When the cats of the second group were confronted with the same escape situation they performed in a manner superior to that of cats in a group which were not afforded an opportunity to observe the escape problem (23).

A study of bilateral transfer contains more evidence that so-called motor learning might be termed "cognitive motor learning." A group of human subjects received practice in a one-handed manipulative task, and then were asked to perform the same task with the other hand. As expected, bilateral transfer occurred; skill acquisition by the second hand was apparently facilitated by the activities of the initial practice. In this same experiment, however, a second group of subjects were permitted to *observe* the first group of subjects practicing the one-handed task, and then were required to demonstrate their own proficiency in the experimental skill. The data revealed that as much skill was evidenced by the second group of subjects who engaged in silent, immobile observation of the skill as was demonstrated by the first group of subjects who had the opportunity to engage in physical practice of the skill with their other hand (11).

Findings of this nature are sometimes explained by suggesting that some kind of muscular activity (a trace response) always accompanies silent thought, and that this muscular activity occurs in the muscle groups that correspond to the activity about which the individual is thinking. In truth, however, it has been demonstrated that individuals may think about movement without muscular responses of any kind occurring (15).

Tolman's cognitive map theory, outlined in the 1930s, was derived from the fact that animals learned the general conformations of mazes independent of movements made when traversing them (41). Some contemporary theorists espousing the overriding importance of movement in the formation of the intellect seem to refute the ability of humans to think without chaining together movement responses and without depending upon a background of successful motor experiences (24).

Proponents of various cognitive theories of learning, however, are more likely to be receptive to the findings emanating from experiments that explore the effects of mental practice upon motor skill. These investigations have usually demonstrated that thinking about a skill, combined with some physical practice, is more helpful than either physical or mental practice alone (12).

A recently published investigation of mental practice illustrates just *when* during the learning process mental practice should be engaged in. Stebbins discovered that mental practice during the initial stages of skill acquisition was as helpful as was physical practice during this same period of time (40). The work of Fleishman and his colleagues substantiates the fact that intellectual and perceptual processes are more important during the initial stages of motor learning than are the motor factors; while during the final stages of learning, such attributes as reaction time and movement speed contribute to a greater proportion to the performance levels attained (13, 14).

Various types of ideomotor training have been engaged in by European athletes participating in sports, with successful results. Team sport athletes have been taught tactics. The success of slalom skiers has been enhanced by aiding them to better learn the nature of the courses that they are to traverse, while athletes engaging in the triple jump have improved their efforts by mentally rehearsing the movements in the event for a period of months (42) in addition to engaging in actual physical practice.

A study just completed by Doctors Rarick and Broadhead using retarded children as subjects elucidates just how engaging in movement tasks may positively affect I.Q. scores of children (31). While earlier studies of this problem area have sometimes employed traditional physical education fitness and recreational activities, this more recent investigation encouraged the children to solve movement problems (40, 34). Children were often placed in pairs and asked to discover several ways of jumping over a line. With this kind of cognitive "exercise" a significant improvement in an I.Q. test involving picture identification was elicited from the experimental subjects, as contrasted to the test scores collected from the control subjects.

A theory of teaching that relates cognition to movement experiences has been advanced by Muska Mosston at Rutgers University. The spectrum of teaching styles advocated by Mosston is exerting a positive influence upon physical education and general education, as children are brought from a situation in which they simply respond to the command of the teachers to a stage in which they are encouraged to solve problems through movement (31).

In a recent monograph some of Mosston's ideas have been incorporated into a series of movement tasks through which retarded and immature children may be encouraged to lengthen their attention spans, to recognize geometric patterns and letters, to improve serial memory abilities, to spell and to count. With further research applications of Mosston's theory to other types of educational, industrial and military situations should be forthcoming (10).

Arguments for the fact that all learning is based upon the quality of the early motor responses seen in infants and in children have come from various sources during the past several years. Piaget argues for the importance of an initial sensory-motor period which purportedly undergrids later cognitive development (36). Newell C. Kephart, a psychologist, has also proposed a perceptual-motor theory which suggests that motor activity contributes in a positive way to the development of perceptual and cognitive processes (24). Piaget suggests that early infantile reflexes somehow blend into voluntary movements, whereas Kephart writes that movement activities aid in the organization of near and distant space (36, 24).

Others, on the other hand, argue against such a simplistic view of child development. Ausubel and Peiper present evidence that most infant reflexes disappear prior to the emergence of voluntary movement attributes (3, 35). Illingworth presents a more tenable theory of child development in which a concept of differentiation of attributes is discussed (17). Illingworth's schema suggests that as children mature their attribute patterns become more diffuse, making it less likely that various mental, motor and perceptual scores will correlate highly with one another.

Meyers and Dingman, after conducing a survey of factoral studies find that mental and motor traits reside in different domains by the age of two years, while innumerable studies have demonstrated the inability to predict later intelligence by scores in motor ability tests administered during the first years of life (25, 5).

Findings from studies of atypical children lacking movement attributes from birth similarly argue against the sweeping generalization that movement is the basis of the intellect. Surveys of perceptual and motor attributes of thalidomide children and of children afflicted with cerebral palsy reveal that often they evidence intellects comparable to the capacities of normal children (2). Often, superior intelligence scores are obtained from children of this nature.

A review of the available material in child development relative to mental-motor relationships suggests that as children mature they develop along several channels simultaneously. Some of these channels, such as scribbling, involve some type of movement attribute, while other channels evolve independent of movements of the larger skeletal muscles. Children can silently sit and think, and can manipulate their environments vicariously as well as directly. A recent investigation by Nancy Bayley, for example, found that the relatively immobile baby who does more looking than moving is likely to produce higher scores on intelligence tests in adolescence and adulthood than will the infant who is more physically active in the first year of life (4).

SUMMARY

The available evidence suggests that "motor" represents only a facet of the human personality. Lemurs living twenty-three million years ago evidenced superior manipulative abilities; most animals can run and jump and engage in more spectacular locomotor behaviors than can humans. Only in the human, however, is found the large associational areas constituting about 90 percent of the neurocortex (26, 30).

It is perhaps because of this relatively recent appearance of structures which mediate high level thought in humans that they have difficulty at times in coordinating thought with motor skill, and why, sometimes, excess preoccupation with mechanical principles on the part of the performer will sometimes interfere with smooth motor output.

Future directions for research seem endless within this general problem area. Correlative as well as causal studies should prove valuable. It is apparent that as one increases the complexity of motor tasks presented to groups, increasingly higher correlations will be found between I.Q. scores and the measures of motor performance collected. The exact manner in which thought-provoking movement education programs contribute to the acquisition of what cognitive abilities, however, remains somewhat obscure at the present time.

Further research should also be concerned with how mental rehearsal interacts with tasks of various levels of difficulty. When and how sports performers and industrial workers should be encouraged to think about the execution of skills important to each provides another interesting avenue of study.

It is apparent that man is both a thinking and a moving animal. The exact conditions under which both facets of his personality may be supportive or disruptive of one another, however, still remains somewhat obscure. To ignore the role of cognitive processes in the acquisition of skill seems as naive as attempting to improve reading by walking balance beams.

BIBLIOGRAPHY

1. ————: Doman-Delacato treatment of neurologically handicapped children. American Academy of Pediatrics Executive Board Statement, *AAP News Letter, 16*:11, 1965.
2. ABERCROMBIE, M. L. J.; GARDINER, P. A.; HANSEN, E.; JONCKHEERE, J.; LINDON, R. L.; SOLOMON, G., AND TYSON, M. C.: Visual, perceptual and visuomotor impairment in physically handicapped children. *Percept Motor Skills, 18*:561-625, 1964.
3. AUSUBEL, D. P.: A critique of Piaget's theory of the ontogenesis of motor behavior. *J Genet Psychol, 109*:119-122, 1966.
4. BAYLEY, NANCY: Behavioral correlates of mental growth—birth to thirty-six years. *Amer Psychol, 23*(1):1-17, 1968.

5. BLOOM, B. S.: *Stability and Change in Human Characteristics.* New York, Wiley, 1964.
6. CORDER, W. D.: Effects of physical education on the intellectual, physical and social development of educable mentally retarded boys. Unpublished special project. Nashville, George Peabody College, 1965.
7. CRATTY, B. J.: *Developmental Sequences of Perceptual-Motor Tasks: Movement Activities for Neurologically Handicapped and Retarded Children and Youth.* Freeport, Long Island, Educational Activities, 1967.
8. CRATTY, B. J.: *Learning and Playing: Fifty Games for Children with Learning Difficulties.* Freeport, Long Island, Educational Activities, 1967.
9. CRATTY, B. J.: *Movement Behavior and Motor Learning,* 2nd ed. Philadelphia, Lea & F., 1967.
10. CRATTY, B. J.: *Movement, Perception and Thought.* Palo Alto, Peek Publications, 1969.
11. EBERHARD, U.: Transfer of training related to finger dexterity. *Percept Motor Skills, 17:*274, 1963.
12. EGSTROM, G.: The effects of an emphasis on conceptualizing techniques upon the early learning of a gross motor skill. Doctoral dissertation, Department of Physical Education, University of Southern California, Los Angeles, California, 1961.
13. FLEISHMAN, E. A., AND HEMPEL, W. E., JR.: Factorial analysis of complex psychomotor performance and related skills. *J Appl Psychol, 40:*2, 1956.
14. FLEISHMAN, E. A., AND RICH S.: Role of kinesthetic and spatial-visual abilities in perceptual-motor learning. *J Exp Psychol, 66:*6-11, 1963.
15. HARDYCK, C. D.: The functions of sub-vocal speech. *Project Literary Reports, 8:*112-115, 1967.
16. HUMPHREY, J. H.: Comparisons of the use of active games and language workbook exercises as learning media in the development of language understandings with third grade children. *Percept Motor Skills, 21:*23-26, 1965.
17. ILLINGWORTH, R. S.: *The Development of the Infant and Young Child, Normal and Abnormal,* Edinburgh, E. & S. Livingstone Ltd., 1967.
18. ISMAIL, A. H., AND GRUBER, J. J.: *Motor Aptitude and Intellectual Performance.* Columbus, Merrill, C. E., 1967.
19. ISMAIL, A. H., AND KIRKENDALL, D. R.: Relationships among three domains of development. Speech presented to the Second International Congress of Sport Psychology, Washington, D. C., Nov. 1968.

20. JACOBSON, E.: *Anxiety and Tension Control—a Physiological Approach.* Philadelphia, Lippincott, 1964.

21. JACOBSEN, E.: *Progressive Relaxation,* 2nd ed. Chicago, U. of Chicago, 1938.

22. JACOBSEN, E.: *Tension in Medicine.* Springfield, Thomas, 1967.

23. JOHN, E. R.: *Mechanisms of Memory.* New York, Academic, 1967.

24. KEPHART, N. C.: *The Slow Learner in the Classroom.* Columbus, Merrill, C. E., 1960.

25. KERSHNER, J. R.: Doman-Delacato's theory of neurological organization applied with retarded children. *Exceptional Child,* 33:441-450, 1968.

26. LA BARRE, W.: *The Human Animal.* Chicago, U. of Chicago, 1954.

27. LAVERY, J. J.: Retention of a skill following training with and without instructions to retain. *Percept Motor Skills,* 18:275-281, 1964.

28. MACCOBY, ELEANOR E.; DOWLEY, EDITH M., AND HAGEN, J. W.: Activity level and intellectual functioning in normal pre-school children. *Child Develop,* 36:761-769, 1965.

29. MEYERS, C. E., AND DINGMAN, H. F.: The structure of abilities at the preschool ages: hypothesized domains. *Psychol Bull,* 57:514-532, 1960.

30. MILNER, ESTHER: *Human Neural and Behavioral Development.* Springfield, Thomas, 1967.

31. MOSSTON, M.: *Teaching Physical Education from Command to Discovery.* Columbus, Merrill, C. E., 1966.

32. MURPHY, G.: *Human Potentialities.* New York, Basic Books, 1958.

33. OLIVER, J. N.: The effects of physical conditioning exercises and activities on the mental characteristics of educationally sub-normal boys. *Brit J Educ Psychol,* 28:155-165, 1958.

34. OLSON, W. C.: *Child Development.* Boston, Heath, 1959.

35. PEIPER, A.: *Cerebral Function in Infancy and Childhood.* New York, Consultants Bureau, 1963.

36. PIAGET, J.: *The Psychology of Intelligence.* Patterson, New Jersey, Littlefield, 1963.

37. RARICK, G. L., AND BROADHEAD, G. D.: The effects of individualized versus group oriented physical education programs on selected parameters of the development of educable mentally retarded, and minimally brain injured children. Monograph sponsored by U. S. Office of Education. Department of Physical Education, University of Wisconsin, Madison, Wisconsin, 1968.

38. ROBBINS, M. P., AND GLASS, G. V.: The Doman-Delacato rationale: a critical analysis. In Jerome Hellmuth (Ed.): *Educational Therapy.* Seattle, Special Child, 1968.

39. SOLOMAN, A., AND PRANGLE, R.: Demonstrations of physical fitness improvement in the EMR. *Exceptional Child,* 33:177-181, 1967.

40. STEBBINS, R. J.: Relationship between the perception and reproduction of certain motor skills. *Res Quart Amer Ass Health Phys Educ,* 39:3, 1968.
41. TOLMAN, E. C.: *Purposeful Behavior in Animals and Men.* New York, Century, 1932.
42. VANEK, M., AND CRATTY, B. J.: *Psychology and the Superior Athlete.* New York, Macmillan, 1970.

Chapter VI

ACTIVITY LEVELS IN CHILDREN AND THE ELEMENTARY SCHOOL CURRICULA

T HROUGH THE YEARS researchers have investigated various relationships, causal and otherwise, between movement and learning. One of the most intriguing lines of study has recently emerged in the writings of several scholars in the United States and Europe which points to the various important hypotheses concerning the manner in which classroom functioning may interact with needs and capacities for movement in children (15, 20, 21).

It is beginning to appear that success in school on the part of children in early and middle childhood may depend upon the extent to which their activity levels coincide with the manner in which "business" is conducted in their classrooms. It is becoming increasingly apparent that school success may be based to a large extent on the manner in which the maturing child can remain physically passive when he is confronted with the relatively static learning tasks found in the average American school.

A brief review of some of the research findings which support these assumptions might help to clarify the above statements.

Eleanor Maccoby and her colleagues, in a study published a few years ago, found moderate to high correlations between measures of impulse control obtained from normal youngsters and scores on tests of I.Q. and academic achievement. The tasks that Maccoby used required that the children move as slowly as they were able in various ways, such as in writing, in walking and the like. She suggested that the children who could place themselves under the strictest control were those who could perform well on standardized tests of intellectual achievement (18).

It is apparent, however, that stable intellectual or emotional functioning is not simply based upon how slow and "under-aroused" a child can make himself, but is based upon the extent to which he can adjust his level of arousal to the demands of the task. A well-functioning child can thus be expected to "get himself up" for participation in playground activities and then quickly lower his level of activation when returning to the classroom immediately afterward (8, 16, 25).

On the other hand, the child who cannot adjust his level of arousal to levels appropriate to various conditions which confront him may be handicapped when attempting to learn (16). In a recently published study carried out in connection with our laboratory a moderate negative correlation of -0.57 was obtained between some of the same impulse control measures employed by Maccoby *et al.* and tests of spelling and reading using twenty-nine Negro children between the ages of six and nine years with I.Q.'s under 80, a mean of 75. In short, the findings of this second investigation indicated that perhaps the reason these children were not learning well was that they habitually maintained a level of arousal too low for adequate classroom functioning. They evidenced not only the inclination to walk lines extremely slowly, but also seemed to form perceptual and cognitive judgments in the same lethargic ways.

The findings of studies by Courts and Freeman in the 1930's, and more recently those emanating from investigations by Dr. Torbjorn Stockfelt and his colleagues in Stockholm, similarly reflect the principle that optimum activation is necessary for good intellectual functioning (3, 8, 15). In these early investigations, raising the subjects' tension levels by asking them to squeeze hand-held grips (dynomometers) at about one half the maximum force of which they were capable resulted in the best scores on tests of memorization which were engaged in at the same time (3, 8). Stockfelt similarly found that the best scores were obtained from subjects who were presented math problems auditorily at the same time that they were running a treadmill at about 45 percent of their maximum capacities (15). The scores on tasks of arithmetic computation produced during this optimum activation period were superior to the scores obtained from the subjects either when they were at rest or when they were running at a pace faster than about one-half maximum capacity.

Among the most interesting research data bearing on the problems of activation, learning, physical capacity and physical need have been recently published by Willie Railo in Norway (20). His findings seem to indicate that if educators succeed in "deactivating" fit children by confining them to the classroom for prolonged periods of time, the "energy" that they will bring to bear upon intellectual tasks may be inhibited to a marked degree. In support of this hypothesis, Railo, by using a work capacity test of physiological fitness, separated 203 children ranging in age from ten to twelve years into two groups: in one group were children who evidenced low fitness levels, and in the other group were children who scored in the upper levels of fitness. Railo and his colleagues then gave both groups standardized I.Q. tests for a period of two hours and following a brief break they subjected both groups to two hours of intensive intellectual endeavor. Following this second two-hour period both groups were again given a comparable but different I.Q. test. The children whose fitness levels were high produced mean scores that were significantly lower than the first scores they obtained prior to the mental work, whereas the I.Q. scores of the less fit children did not drop at the second testing but remained the same!

Railo concluded that the children with high fitness levels experienced psychological discomfort during the prolonged periods of confined mental work, accompanied perhaps by high needs for activity. General inhibition had built up in the situation described which reflected negatively when they were asked to again perform intellectually. The children with low fitness levels, it was hypothesized, experienced no frustration of their activity needs, as their needs for movement were not very great. The members of this second group thus were somehow able to maintain a relatively stable level of mental work throughout the six-hour test-work-test period during which the investigation was conducted.

A program of research carried out by Petri has produced other evidence which relates to the topic under discussion (19). Using tests of pain tolerance, kinesthetic sensitivity and visual sensitivity, she concluded that individuals may be classified into two general perceptual types. One type is the "reducer" of stimuli, the energetic, active and relatively insensitive individual evidencing a high pain threshold, this usually being the male. The other type is the "augmenter" of stimuli. This individual can be counted upon to be extremely sensitive to input, to remain relatively passive and to process information rather than to generate output. E. Dean Ryan has verified Petri's findings, and suggests furthermore that there are perceptual characteristics evidenced by vigorous people which are at variance with the perceptual characteristics exhibited by the more passive (23).

Further evidence relating activity level to classroom functioning suggests that in all cases in which the activity level of poor readers and underachievers in school is measured and compared to academically superior children, the poor readers and underachievers are more active.* Kagan and others have confirmed the expected by finding a relationship between body-build and physical impulsivity (14). The more muscular child is generally more prone to utilize his muscular capacities, or in possessing a high need for movement a child may inevitably acquire a well-developed system of skeletal musculature. Taken together these findings point to several general principles which in turn could lead to various courses of action on the parts of educators.

1. There are many generally active children whose habitual ways of behaving are not compatible with protocols currently employed in classroom teaching.*

------

* Activity levels in children can be measured in a number of ways, including clocking attention span in the classroom, random activity in rooms crossed by grids or by electric eyes, by force platforms registering movement in chairs, or by cameras recording movements in various environments, or within activity rooms in which various toys are wired to record participation.

* By "generally active" it is not meant that children are evidencing some kind of organic and/or emotional problem resulting in what has been termed the "hyperkinetic syndrome." However, it is apparent that children's activity levels may be arranged on a continuum from those extremely passive, through the middle portions of the scale in which children with high activity needs might be placed, to the pathological end of the continuum in which the neurologically impaired and/or emotionally disturbed children should be fixed.

2. Hyperactivity interferes with learning.
3. Active people may possess different capacities for and competencies in perceptual and learning tasks.
4. There is a desirable level of activation necessary for a given task, which if either not reached or exceeded will result in less than optimum performance. This principle is valid for either mental or motor tasks.

There are two basic tactics which educators have employed in dealing with active children in school. Rousseau and more contemporary educators have at times constructed learning experiences which have involved physical activity by children (7, 22). A recent text by Cratty contains ways in which total body movement may be used to enhance various components of classroom functioning, including pattern recognition, spelling, letter recognition and skills in mathematics (5). James Humphrey and others have paired traditional classroom learning experiences with movement and achieved good results (10).

A second tactic is to attempt to reduce the activity levels of the children being dealt with. Literature from Czechoslovakia and from recent investigations in this country have confirmed the fact that reduction of activity, the lowering of indices of physiological arousal, the lengthening of attention spans and the heightening of motor and mental competencies is possible through the application of various structured programs of relaxation and impulse control training (1, 2, 9, 12, 13, 24).*

It is probable, however, that in truth some combination of both tactics would be the most useful approach. While it is not realistic to expect curricula to change radically in content, it is believed that generally fit and active children will benefit, particularly during their early years, with the introduction of more active learning experiences into the curricula. At the same time many children should be given help in obtaining better self-control. Many adult occupations require passivity rather

---

* This training advanced by Jacobson, Schultz and others consists of alternately tightening and relaxing muscles, in groups and totally, as well as deep-breathing exercises accompanied by verbal suggestions to relax, or whatever verbal imagery is appropriate to the maturational level of the subjects involved.

than constant motion; mature functioning in our society is marked by a reduction of activity level. To simply activate already active youngsters with a program composed of active learning games is also not realistic.

It is believed, however, that if children are given opportunities to vent their needs for movement through participation in vigorous activity, then when they are later asked to redirect their energies into intellectual tasks this vigorous activity will have proven helpful. Unfortunately, there is little information concerning the optimum number of recess periods, the lengths of these recess periods and the amounts of vigorous action which would be productive of maximum classroom learning on the parts of normal children. In any case, studies of this nature should attempt to isolate individual differences in activity and fitness levels evidenced by the participating subjects in order that valid inferences may be drawn from the data.

In conclusion it is suggested that physical activity needs and capacities on the parts of elementary school children will not necessarily interfere with academic learning unless the learning environment is too restrictive in nature. The goal, I believe, should not be to produce passive inactive and unfit children whose personalities may match the traditional environment, but should be made to match the individual differences in activity needs and capacities in children with various educational strategies. A child should be encouraged to express and to develop both his capacities and his skills in movement as well as his capacities for cognitive functions. The success of the elementary school curriculum, I believe, will to a large degree be dependent upon the extent to which these two facets of the child's personality are welded together by a congruent set of learning experiences.

BIBLIOGRAPHY

1. ALLEN, K. E.; HENKE, L. B.; HARRIS, F. R.; BAER, D. M., AND REYNOLDS, N. J.: Control of hyperactivity by social reinforcement of attending behavior. *J Educ Psychol, 58*:231-237, 1967.
2. BEDNAROVA, V.: An investigation concerning the influence of psychotonic exercise upon the indices of concentration of attentiveness. *Teor Prax Teles Vychov, 16*(7):437-442, 1968.

3. COURTS, F. A.: Relation Between Experimentally Induced Muscular Tension and Memorization. *J Exp. Psychol, 170*(25):235-256, 1939.

4. CRATTY, BRYANT J.: *Perceptual-Motor Behavior and Educational Processes.* Springfield, Thomas, 1969.

5. CRATTY, BRYANT J.: *Perception, Movement and Thought.* Palo Alto, Peek Publications, 1969.

6. DUFFY, ELIZABETH: *Activation and Behavior.* New York, Wiley, 1962.

7. FERNALD, GRACE M., AND KELLER, HELEN: The effects of kinesthetic factors in the development of word recognition in the case of non-readers. *J Educ Res, 4*:355-376, 1921.

8. FREEMAN, G. L.: Changes in tonus during completed and interrupted mental work. *J Gen Psychol, 170*(4):309-334, 1930.

9. HARRISON, WADE; LECRONE, HAROLD; TEMERLIN, M. K., AND TROUSDALE, W.: The effect of music and exercise upon the self-help skills of non-verbal retardates. *American J Ment Defic, 71*:279-282, 1966.

10. HUMPHREY, J. H.: Comparisons of the use of active games and language workbook exercises as learning media in the development of language understandings with third grade children. *Percept Motor Skills, 21*:23-26, 1965.

11. JACOBSON, E.: *Anxiety and Tension Control—a Physiologic Approach.* Philadelphia, Lippincott, 1964.

12. JACOBSON, E.: *Progressive Relaxation,* 2nd ed. Chicago, U. of Chicago, 1938.

13. JOHNSON, DALE I., AND SPIELBERGER, C. D.: The effects of relaxation training and the passage of time on measures of static and trait anxiety. *J Clin Psychol, 24*:20-23, 1968.

14. KAGAN, JEROME: Body build and conceptual impulsivity in children. *J Personality, 34*:118-128, 1966.

15. KRONBY, BO: How a person's numerical ability is changed, during different loads of physical work on an ergometric bicycle. Report from Pedagogisk-Psykologiska Institutionen Vid GIH, Stockholm, October, 1968.

16. LAUFER, M. W.; DENHOFF, E., AND SOLOMONS, G.: Hyperkinetic impulse disorder in children's behavior problems. *Psychosom Med, 19*:38-49, 1957.

17. LYNN, R.: *Attention, Arousal and the Orientation Reaction.* New York, Pergamon, 1966.

18. MACCOBY, ELEANOR E.; DOWLEY, EDITH M., AND HAGEN, JOHN W.: Activity level and intellectual functioning in normal pre-school children. *Child Develop, 36*:761-769, 1965.

19. PETRI, ASENATH: *Individuality in Pain and Suffering.* Chicago, U. of Chicago, 1967.

20. RAILO, WILLI S.: Physical fitness and intellectual achievement. A

Monograph, Norwegian College of Physical Education and Sport, 1968.

21. RAILO, WILLI S.: Physical and mental endurance. A Preliminary Report, Norwegian College of Physical Education and Sport, 1967.

22. ROUSSEAU, JACQUES: *Emile on Education.* Trans. by Holland, Lucy E., and Turner, Francis C. Syracuse, Bardeen, C. W., 1915.

23. RYAN, E. DEAN: Perceptual characteristics of vigorous people. In Brown, Roscoe C., and Cratty, Bryant J. (Eds.): *New Perspectives of Man in Action.* Englewood Cliffs, New Jersey, Prentice-Hall, 1969.

24. SCHULTZ, J. H.: *Das Autogenne Training, Konzentrative Selbstentspannung* (The Self Training, The Concentrative Self-Relaxation). Stuttgart, 1956.

25. ZEAMAN, D., AND HOUSE, BETTY J.: The role of attention in retardate discrimination learning. In Ellis, N. R. (Ed.): *Handbook of Mental Deficiency.* New York, McGraw, 1963.

Chapter VII

READING AND THE ROLE OF MOTOR TRAINING*

T HE JARGON EMPLOYED by various "educationalists" purporting to remediate learning problems, including reading by employing some type of perceptual-motor panacea, is often inexact, naive and at times downright misleading. Educationalists may suggest, for example, that "movement is the basis of the intellect," and at other times that "something vaguely referred to as 'perceptual development' is enhanced by walking the balance beam." In direct statements, and at other times through subtle inferences, they suggest that by religiously following some kind of stylized program of "sensory-motor, perceptual-motor, motor-perceptual, or motor-sensory" ritual, reading problems are likely to be eradicated (11, 12, 18).

This type of statement needs to be carefully examined and critically evaluated. For often, while these pronouncements contain some apparently self-evident truths, they usually are heavily permeated with logical fallacies, as well as presenting "facts" which are at odds with the available experimental findings.

It is true that behavior of all types involves movement, for indeed the terms are synonymous. It is true that a child's eyes move from word to word while he reads. However, it is also true that these fixations occur at the rate of from 3 to 5 per second, well beyond the realm of voluntary control. It is thus doubtful that these eye movements can be improved through training or otherwise modified by any kind of visual or visual-motor training (3, 7, 29, 30).

It is also apparent that hyperactive children, unable to

---

* Speech presented to the "Understanding Poor Reader" Conference, University of California, Los Angeles, May 17-18, 1969.

163

control the incidence of their bodily movements, cannot usually read well, as they seem unable to give their attention to a printed page for a period of time long enough to elicit understanding of just what word shapes translate to what verbal-cognitive symbols. It may also be true that in these children, some kind of neuromotor "spillover" from the truncal muscles to the eye muscles is occurring which prevents them from fixating their eyes on the page in an efficient fashion while their bodies wriggle in their schoolroom chairs (10, 10, 32).

At the same time, it is equally true that reading is a complex process in which success is dependent upon verbal, cognitive and visual attributes. Thus, to suggest that some kind of training of peripheral functions, i.e. motor coordination or vision, will improve the total complex process of word-shape translation is an oversimplification of an extremely complex procedure.

In essence, the research findings which bear upon relationships between reading and motor functioning may be summarized as follows:

1. The highest correlations between reading scores and motor proficiency are generally obtained when balance measures are employed, and do not usually exceed +.4 (7). Thus the variance in the separate measures remaining unaccounted for is considerably more than that explained by the correlation. Even this slight correlation, of course, does not infer causality, and probably simply indicates that some similar kind of ocular efficiency is needed both in tasks involving static and dynamic balance and when moving the eye across a page in reading.

2. Within groups of poor readers one is likely to find two subgroups: one consisting of children who evidence only verbal-linguistic problems, and a second comprised of children who may be described as exhibiting classic dyslexia (i.e. evidencing concomitant motor, perceptual and reading impairment) (9).

3. The findings arising from causal studies in which the effects of programs of perceptual-motor training have been assessed as influential in reading are generally not very promising. For example, the Kephart program has

been evaluated by several scholars who have been forced to conclude that while the program positively influenced certain perceptual-motor characteristics inherent in the training, it exerted no effect upon reading proficiency.* (6, 19, 24, 26). Similar results have been obtained when the Delacato program has been scrutinized via the experimental method (7, 25, 31).

4. Research surveying the effect of visual-motor training espoused by the Optometric Extension Program is not plentiful and of dubious quality. One study, for example, contains three subjects (21), a second is disseminated in mimeographed form with a commercially produced training manual (22), while a third researcher has made no attempt to treat his data with any degree of statistical sophistication (13). Proponents of this type of training have generally failed to prove that visual training exerts any positive influence upon *ocular function* prior to examining the influence of visual training upon academic achievement.

At the same time it is believed that a well-designed program of physical education can have a beneficial effect upon certain children with learning problems. For example, the available data suggests that . . .

1. Movement will aid intelligence to the extent to which the child is encouraged to think about the movements in which he is engaged (8, 15).

2. Certain movement activities may aid in the improvement of specific perceptual traits, but must be certain to teach for the transfer from motor to perceptual traits (14).

3. The extent to which we may aid a child to control his own activity may reduce hyperactivity, which in turn may be interfering with the learning of a number of classroom tasks (1, 16).

4. A general failure-set elicited by ineptitude in playground

---

* It is not believed, however, that the worth of the Kephart program as part of a prereading program has been thoroughly researched using preschool children as subjects.

games may transfer to other educational tasks (8, 32).
5. Failure to guide the hand efficiently when writing will contribute to inefficient classroom performance, as the child is unable to transcribe his thoughts to paper (8, 27).
6. Training in rhythmic perception may contribute to early success in reading (17, 28).

There is no evidence, however, that a vaguely defined group of poor or nonreaders will be significantly improved by exposure to tasks involving the use of the larger skeletal muscles. Reading and causes for reading failure are probably as numerous as the causes for mental retardation itself.* Only by carefully assessing individual differences in self-concept, activity level and motor proficiency can we be expected to offer direct and indirect help to children with learning problems by exposure to structured and/or unstructured programs of physical activity.

BIBLIOGRAPHY

1. ALLEN, K. E.; HENKE, L. B.; HARRIS, F. R.; BAER, D. M., AND REYNOLDS, N. J.: Control of hyperactivity by social reinforcement of attending behavior. *J Educ Psychol, 58*:231-237, 1967.
2. AMBLE, B. R., *et al.*: Perceptual span training and reading achievement of school children. *J Educ Psychol, 57*:192-206, 1966.
3. ANDERSON, I. H.: Studies in the eye movements of good and poor readers. *Psychol Monogr, 48*(3), 1937.
4. BELMONT, L., AND BIRCH, H. G.: Lateral dominance, lateral awareness, and reading disability. *Child Develop, 36*:57-71, 1965.
5. BENDER, L.: In Kennedy, A. H., and Kenney, V. T. (Eds.): *Dyslexia.* St. Louis, Mosby, 1968, pp. 75-76.
6. BROWN, R. C.: The effect of a perceptual-motor education program on perceptual-motor skills and reading readiness. Presented at Research Section, AAHPER, St. Louis, April 1, 1968.
7. CRATTY, B. J.: . . . of muscles and reading. In *Some Educational Implications of Movement Experiences.* Seattle, Special Child, 1970.
8. CRATTY, B. J., AND MARTIN, SISTER MARGARET MARY: *Perceptual-motor Efficiency in Children, The Measurement and Improvement of Movement Attributes.* Philadelphia, Lea & F., 1969.

---

* Estimated by some to number somewhere between 70 and 80.

9. CRAWLEY, J. F.; GOODSTEIN, H. A., AND BURROW, W. H.: *Reading and Psychomotor Disability Among Mentally Retarded and Average Children.* Storrs, Conn., School of Education, University of Conn., 1968.

10. CROMWELL, R. L.; BAUMEISTER, A., AND HAWKINS, W. F.: Research in activity level. In *Handbook of Mental Deficiency.* New York, McGraw, 1963, 632-663.

11. DELACATO, C. H.: *Treatment and Prevention of Reading Problems.* Springfield, Thomas, 1963.

12. GETMAN, G. N., AND KANE, E. R.: *The Physiology of Readiness: An An Action Program for the Development of Perception for Children,* Minneapolis, P.A.S.S., Inc., 1964.

13. HALGREN, M. R.: Opus in see sharp. *Education, 1*:369-371, 1961.

14. HILL, S. D.; McCULLUM, A. H., AND SCEAN, A.: Relation of training in motor activity to development of left-right directionality in mentally retarded children: exploratory study. *Percept Motor Skills, 24*:363-366, 1967.

15. HUMPHREY, J. H.: Comparison of the use of active games and language workbook exercises as learning media in the development of language understandings with third grade children. *Percept Motor Skills, 21*:23-26, 1965.

16. JOHNSON, D. I., AND SPIELBERGER, C. D.: The efforts of relaxation training and the passage of time on measures of state and trait anxiety. *J Chem Psych, 24*:21-23, 1968.

17. KATZ, P. A., AND DEUTSCH, M.: Modality of stimulus presentation in serial learning for retarded and normal readers. *Percept Motor Skills, 19*:627-633, 1964.

18. KEPHART, N. C.: Perceptual-motor aspects of learning disabilities. *Exceptional Child, 31*:201-206, 1964.

19. LAPRAY, M., AND ROSS, R.: Auditory and visual-perceptual training. In Figurel, J. A. (Ed.): *Vistas in Reading.* International Reading Association Conference Proceedings, XI, 1966, 530-532.

20. LYNN, R. P.: Individual difference in introversion-extroversion, reactive inhibition and reading attainment. *J Educ Psychol, 51*:318-321, 1960.

21. LYONS, C. V., AND LYONS, E. B.: The power of visual training as measured in factors of intelligence. *J Amer Optom Ass,* Dec., 1954, 255-262.

22. MACCOBY, E. E.; DOWLEY, E. M., AND HAGEN, J. W.: Activity level and intellectual functioning in normal pre-school children. *Child Develop, 36*:761-769, 1965.

23. McCORMICK, C. C.; POETGER, B. S.; JANICO, N., AND FOOTLICK, S. W.: *Improvement in Reading Achievement Through Perceptual-Motor Training.* Chicago, Reading Research Foundation, Inc., 1967.

24. ROACH, E. G.: Evaluation of an experimental program of perceptual-motor training with slow readers. In Figurel, J. A. (Ed.): *Vistas in Reading.* International Reading Association Conference Proceedings, XI, 1966.

25. ROBBINS, M. P.: A study of the validity of Delacato's theory of neurological organization. *Exceptional Child, 32*:617-623, 1966.

26. RUTHERFORD, W. L.: Perceptual-motor training and readiness. In Figurel, J. A. (Ed.): *Redding and Inquiry.* International Reading Association Conference Proceedings, X, 1965, 194-196.

27. SMITH, C., AND KEOGH, B.: The group Bender Gestalt as a reading readiness screening instrument. *Percept Motor Skills, 15*:639-645, 1962.

28. STERRITT, G. M., AND RUDNICK, M.: Auditory and visual rhythm perception in relation to reading ability in fourth grade boys. *Percept Motor Skills, 22*:859-864, 1966.

29. TAYLOR, S. E.: Eye movements in reading, facts and fallacies. *Amer Educ Res J, 2*:187-201, 1965.

30. TINKER, M. A.: Recent studies of eye movement in reading. *Psychol Bull, 55*:215-231, 1958.

31. YARBOROUGH, B. H.: A study of the effectiveness of the Leavell Language-Development Service in improving the silent reading ability and other language skills of persons with mixed dominance. Charlottesville, University of Virginia, doctoral thesis, 1964.

32. ZEAMAN, D., AND HOUSE, B. J.: The role of attention in retardate discrimination learning. In Ellis, N. R. (Ed.): *Handbook of Mental Deficiency.* New York, McGraw, 1963, 159-223.

APPENDIX

SELF-CONCEPT TEST

Name .... Age .... Sex ....

Evaluated by .... Date....................

Questions: (Ask child to circle yes or no only.)

1.	Are you good at making things with your hands	yes	no
2.	Can you draw well?	yes	no
3.	Are you strong?	yes	no
4.	Do you like the way you look?	yes	no
5.	Do you friends make fun of you?	yes	no
6.	Are you handsome/pretty?	yes	no
7.	Do you have trouble making friends?	yes	no
8.	Do you like school?	yes	no
9.	Do you wish you were different?	yes	no
10.	Are you sad most of the time?	yes	no
11.	Are you the last to be chosen in games?	yes	no
12.	Do girls like you?	yes	no
13.	Are you a good leader in games and sports?	yes	no
14.	Are you clumsy?	yes	no
15.	In games do you watch instead of play?	yes	no
16.	Do boys like you?	yes	no
17.	Are you happy most of the time?	yes	no
18.	Do you have nice hair?	yes	no
19.	Do you play with younger children a lot?	yes	no
20.	Is reading easy for you?	yes	no

GAMES CHOICE TEST

Name ....Age ....Boy ......Girl ......

1.	Soldiers	Yes	No	19.	Build Forts	Yes	No
2.	House	Yes	No	20.	Toy Trains	Yes	No
3.	Doctors	Yes	No	21.	Darts	Yes	No
4.	Cowboys	Yes	No	22.	Dance	Yes	No
5.	Hunting	Yes	No	23.	Wrestling	Yes	No
6.	Cars	Yes	No	24.	Sewing	Yes	No
7.	Cops and Robbers	Yes	No	25.	See Saw	Yes	No
8.	Wall Dodgeball	Yes	No	26.	Football	Yes	No
9.	Marbles	Yes	No	27.	Dolls	Yes	No
10.	Hopscotch	Yes	No	28.	Bows and Arrows	Yes	No
11.	Use Tools	Yes	No	29.	Shooting	Yes	No
12.	Jump Rope	Yes	No	30.	Jacks	Yes	No
13.	Boxing	Yes	No	31.	Make Model Airplanes	Yes	No
14.	Bowling	Yes	No	32.	Drop the Handkerchief	Yes	No
15.	Bandits	Yes	No	33.	Store	Yes	No
16.	Spaceman	Yes	No	34.	Farmer in the Dell	Yes	No
17.	London Bridge	Yes	No	35.	Ring Around the Rosy	Yes	No
18.	Cooking	Yes	No	36.	Mother May I?	Yes	No
				37.	Musical Chairs	Yes	No

FIGURE DRAWING TEST

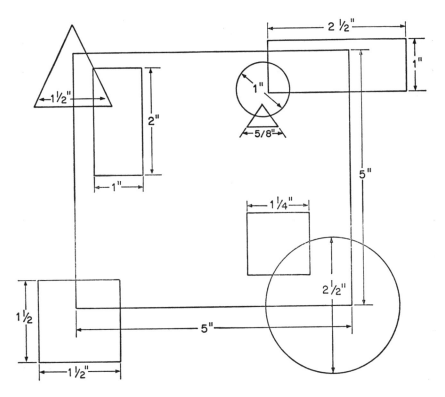

FIGURE DRAWING TEST
SCORE SHEET

	Location of Figure	Accuracy of Figure	Size of Figure
1.			
2.			
3.			
4.			
5.			
6.			
7.			
8.			
9.			
10.			
TOTALS			

INDEX

Impulse control, changes due to
    practice, 132
Inglis, J., 5, 43
Inhibition of movement and intellectual
    performance, 157
Intelligence and fitness, 157
Intelligence and motor behavior, 145
    prediction from early indices of
        motor ability, 150
Intellectual ability and game choices,
    46
Intellectual performance and grip
    tension, 156
I.Q. and activity level in children, 155
    change in motor training, 148
    of retarded children, 146
I.Q., of retarded children, 146
    and self-concept, 7
Ismail, A., 146, 152

J

Jacks, 72
Jacobson, E., 159, 161
Janico, N., 167
Jennett, C., 10
Jersild, A. T., 6, 43
Johnson, D., 167
Johnson, W., 109
Jonckheere, J., 150, 151
Jourard, S. M., 5, 43

K

Kagan, J., 158, 161
Katz, 167
Kellogg, R., 43
Kennedy, A., 166
Kenney, V., 166
Keogh, B., 168
Kephart, N., 86, 108, 109, 110, 111,
    140, 148, 149, 153, 167
Kershner, J., 109, 110, 111, 112, 140
Kinesthetic perception and visual
    perception, 157
Kirkendall, D., 146, 152
Kronby, B., 155, 161

L

LaBarre, W., 150, 153
LaPray, M., 86, 109, 167
Laufer, M., 156, 161
Learning Games, 110, 111
    facilities used, 123
    program procedures, 124
    study, findings, 137
    transfer, 138
Left-right discrimination, change due
    to practice, 105
    in children, 88
    perception of, 91
Leighton, J., 43
Lindon, R., 150, 151
Letter recognition, changes due to
    practicing learning games, 134
    difficult versus easy letters, 120
    tests of, 116
Lowenfeld, M., 45, 48, 85
Lynn, R., 167
Lyons, C., 167
Lyons, E., 167

M

Maccoby, E., 155, 161
Malak, M., ix
Martin, S. M. M., vii, 7, 9, 42, 89,
    108, 110, 140, 166
McCormick, C., 167
McLarren, M., 43
Mental practice of skill, 148
Mental practice and skiing, 148
Meyers, C., 145, 150, 153
Milner, E., 150, 153
Montessori, M., 110, 140
Motivation and academic improvement
    through motor training, 111
Morgan, E., 85
Motor ability and academic
    competencies, correlations, 119
    traits, changes due to practice, 130
Motor activity and perceptual
    organization, 149
Motor learning and cognition, 145
Motor performance and persistence,
    115

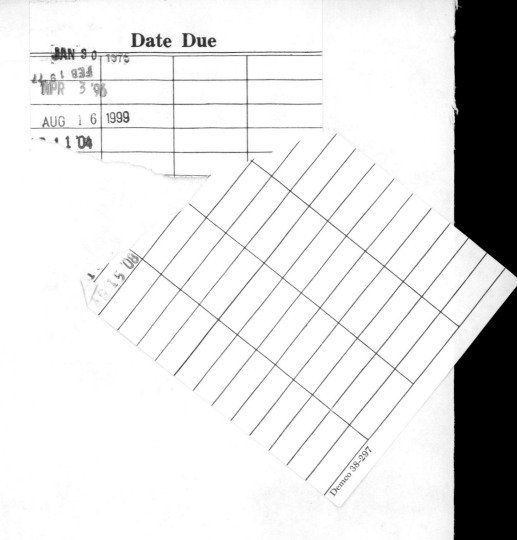